D0198276

Economic Growth

The Lionel Robbins Lectures

Determinants of Economic Growth

A Cross-Country Empirical Study

Robert J. Barro

The MIT Press
Cambridge, Massachusetts
London, England

Second MIT Press paperback edition, 1999

This book was set in Palatino by Windfall Software using ZzTEX.

Printed and bound in the United States of America.

Library of Congress Cataloging-in-Publication Data

Barro, Robert J.
  Determinants of economic growth : a cross-country empirical study
  / Robert J. Barro.
      p.   cm. — (Lionel Robbins lectures)
  Includes bibliographical references and index.
  ISBN 0-262-02421-7 (hc: alk. paper), 0-262-52254-3 (pb)
  1. Economic development—Cross-cultural studies. 2. Economic
policy—Cross-cultural studies. I. Title. II. Series.
HD75.B365   1997
338.9—dc21   96-50235
                                                        CIP

Contents

Foreword

One of the most important questions in economics is, What causes economic growth and thus prosperity for the people of the world? We were therefore delighted when Robert Barro of Harvard University agreed to lecture on this topic for the 1995/96 Lionel Robbins Memorial Lectures delivered at the London School of Economics. He is not only one of the world's leading macroeconomists but has also worked extensively in recent years on the subject of growth.

In the first lecture (chapter 1) he presents his overall analysis. Growth differences between countries depend first on each country's existing level of output. If a country's current output is below its steady-state level of output, there is a catching-up process, which occurs mainly through technology transfer. Each year's growth eliminates some $2^1/2$ percent of the gap between actual and steady-state output. However, this does not mean that poor countries necessarily grow faster than rich ones, or that intercountry inequality necessarily falls over time, for other factors too affect growth, including simple shocks as well as factors producing different steady-state levels of output. To isolate the main determinants of growth, Barro does a careful statistical analysis of growth differences across roughly a hundred countries since 1965. The main factors he identifies as conducive to growth are high levels of schooling, good health (measured by life expectancy), low fertility, low government welfare expenditures, the rule of law, and favorable terms of trade. These findings are of profound importance to everyone concerned with the process of economic reform.

Barro turns in chapter 2 to the issue of democracy. Is it good for growth? Using the same methodology, he concludes that some amount of democracy is better than none, but full democracy may encourage economic distortions, hampering growth. What then determines how democratic a country is? Barro's evidence confirms Lipset's hypothesis that prosperity is good for democracy.

Finally, in his third lecture (chapter 3) he turns to the effect of inflation on growth. He shows clearly that high inflation is bad for growth, but inflation up to 20 percent a year may or may not be.

These lectures are an important contribution to what we know about two of the most important issues of our age: prosperity and freedom. The Lionel Robbins Memorial Trust is extremely grateful to Robert Barro for giving the lectures, which were as good to listen to as they are to read.

Richard Layard
London School of Economics

Preface

The revival of interest in growth theory and empirics is now about ten years old. The initial excitement centered on endogenous growth theories, in which the long-term growth rate was determined by government policies and other forces contained in the analysis. The first models were standard except that capital was broadened to include human components and to allow for spillover effects (Romer 1986, Lucas 1988, Rebelo 1991). In these settings, the absence of diminishing returns meant that the accumulation of capital could sustain growth indefinitely, although the rates of growth and investment might not be Pareto optimal.

Subsequent analyses argued that technological progress generated by the discovery of new ideas was the only way to avoid diminishing returns in the long run. In these models, the purposive behavior that underlay innovations hinged on the prospect of monopoly profits, which provided individual incentives to carry out costly research (Romer 1990, Aghion and Howitt 1992, Grossman and Helpman 1991, chaps. 3, 4). Again, the equilibria need not be Pareto optimal, and there were some intriguing implications for policy, notably for subsidies to basic research.

Despite these breakthroughs, the recent empirical work on growth across countries and regions has not received its main inspiration from the new theories. Rather, the standard applied framework derives more from the older, neoclassical model, as extended to incorporate government policies (including institutional choices that maintain property rights and free markets), accumulation of human capital, fertility decisions, and the diffusion of technology. In particular, the neoclassical model's central idea of conditional convergence receives strong support from the data: poorer countries grow faster per capita once one holds constant measures of government policy, initial levels of human capital, and so on.

Theories of basic technological change are most important for understanding why the world as a whole—and, more specifically, the economies at the technological frontier— can grow in the long run. But these theories have less to do with the determination of relative rates of growth across economies, that is, with the relations studied in cross-country or cross-region statistical analyses. It is surely an irony that one of the lasting contributions of endogenous growth theory is that it stimulated empirical work that demonstrated the explanatory power of the neoclassical growth model.

The first essay begins with a sketch of old and new growth theories. An empirical framework that embodies the idea of conditional convergence is then derived from an extended version of the neoclassical growth model. In this setting, the growth rate depends on the relation between the initial level of output, y, and its target position, y^*. The target, y^*, depends on government policies and on household behavior with respect to saving, work effort, and fertility. For given determinants of y^*, the growth rate varies inversely with y (the conditional convergence effect). For given y, the growth rate increases with y^*—for example, with improved property rights and lower tax rates. In addition, the speed of convergence of y to y^* is increased by a higher starting level of human capital.

The empirical findings for a panel of around a hundred countries strongly support the general notion of conditional convergence. For a given starting level of real per capita gross domestic product (GDP), the growth rate is enhanced by higher initial schooling and life expectancy, lower fertility, lower government consumption, better maintenance of the rule of law, lower inflation, and improvements in the terms of trade. For given values of these and other variables, growth is negatively related to the initial level of real per capita GDP.

The second essay details the interplay between economic development and democracy. The extent of democracy, measured by the role of elections, does not emerge as a critical determinant of growth, but there is some evidence of a nonlinear relationship. At low levels of political rights, an expansion of these rights stimulates economic growth. However, once a moderate amount of democracy has been attained, further expansion reduces growth. A possible interpretation is that, in extreme dictatorships, an increase in political rights tends to raise growth because the limitation on governmental authority is critical. However, in nations that have already achieved some political rights, further democratization may retard growth because of the heightened concern with social programs and income redistribution.

In contrast to the weak effect of democracy on growth, there is a strong positive linkage from prosperity to the propensity to experience democracy, a relation called the Lipset (1959) hypothesis. Various measures of the standard of living—real per capita GDP, life expectancy, and a smaller gap between male and female educational attainment—are found to predict democracy. Additional effects considered include urbanization, natural resources, country size, inequality, colonial history, and religious affiliation.

The final essay details the link between inflation–monetary policy and economic growth. The basic finding is that higher inflation goes along with a lower rate of economic growth. Moreover, the adverse effect of higher inflation on economic outcomes is quantitatively important. This pattern shows up clearly for inflation rates in excess of 15 to 20 percent annually but cannot be isolated statistically for the more moderate experiences. However, there is no evidence in any range of a positive relation between inflation and growth. The analysis also suggests that the estimates isolate the direction of causation from inflation to growth, rather than the reverse.

1   Economic Growth and Convergence

Neoclassical and Endogenous Growth Theories

In the 1960s, growth theory consisted mainly of the neoclassical model, as developed by Ramsey (1928), Solow (1956), Swan (1956), Cass (1965), and Koopmans (1965). One feature of this model, which has been exploited seriously as an empirical hypothesis only in recent years, is the convergence property: the lower the starting level of real per capita gross domestic product (GDP), the higher is the predicted growth rate.

If all economies were intrinsically the same except for their starting capital intensities, then convergence would apply in an absolute sense; that is, poor places would tend to grow faster per capita than rich ones. However, if economies differ in various respects—including propensities to save and have children, willingness to work, access to technology, and government policies—then the convergence force applies only in a conditional sense. The growth rate tends to be high if the starting per capita GDP is low in relation to its long-run or steady-state position, that is, if an economy begins far below its own target position. For example, a poor country that also has a low long-term position, possibly because its public policies are harmful or its saving rate is low, would not tend to grow rapidly.

The convergence property derives in the neoclassical model from the diminishing returns to capital. Economies that have less capital per worker (relative to their long-run capital per worker) tend to have higher rates of return and higher growth rates. The convergence is conditional because the steady-state levels of capital and output per worker depend in the neoclassical model on the propensity to save, the growth rate of population, and the position of the production function—characteristics that may vary across economies. Recent extensions of the model suggest the inclusion of additional sources of cross-country variation, especially government policies with respect to levels of consumption spending, protection of property rights, and distortions of domestic and international markets.

The concept of capital in the neoclassical model can be usefully broadened from physical goods to include human capital in the forms of education, experience, and health. (See Lucas 1988, Rebelo 1991, Caballe and Santos 1993, Mulligan and Sala-i-Martin 1993, and Barro and Sala-i-Martin 1995, chap. 5.) The economy tends toward a steady-state ratio of human to physical capital, but the ratio may depart from its long-run value in an initial state. The extent of this departure generally affects the rate at which per capita output approaches its steady-state value. For example, a country that starts with a high ratio of human to physical capital (perhaps because of a war that destroyed mainly physical capital) tends to grow rapidly because physical capital is more amenable than human capital to rapid expansion. A supporting force is that the adaptation of foreign technologies is facilitated by a large endowment of human capital (see Nelson and Phelps 1966, and Benhabib and Spiegel 1994). This element implies an interaction effect whereby a country's growth rate is more sensitive to its starting level of per capita output the greater is its initial stock of human capital.

Another prediction of the neoclassical model, even when extended to include human capital, is that in the absence of continuing improvements in technology, per capita growth eventually must cease. This prediction, which resembles those of Malthus (1798) and Ricardo (1817), comes from the assumption of diminishing returns to a broad concept of capital. The long-run data for many countries indicate, however, that positive rates of per capita growth can persist over a century or more and that these growth rates have no clear tendency to decline.

Growth theorists of the 1950s and 1960s recognized this modeling deficiency and usually patched it up by assuming that technological progress occurred in an unexplained (exogenous) manner. This device can reconcile the theory with a positive, possibly constant per capita growth rate in the long run, while retaining the prediction of conditional convergence. The obvious shortcoming, however, is that the long-run per capita growth rate is determined entirely by an element—the rate of technological progress—that comes from outside the model. (The long-run growth rate of the level of output depends also on the growth rate of population, another element that is exogenous in the standard theory.) Thus, we end up with a model of growth that explains everything but long-run growth, an obviously unsatisfactory situation.

Recent work on endogenous growth theory has sought to supply the missing explanation of long-run growth. In the main, this approach provides a theory of technical progress, one of the central missing elements of the neoclassical model. The inclusion of a theory of technological change in the neoclassical framework is difficult, however, because the standard competitive assumptions cannot be maintained. (These assumptions work fine in the framework of Frank Ramsey, David Cass, and Tjalling Koopmans.)

Technological advance involves the creation of new ideas, which are partially nonrival and therefore have aspects of public goods. For a given technology—that is, a given state of knowledge—it is reasonable to assume constant returns to scale in the standard, rival factors of production, such as raw labor, broad capital, and land. But then the returns to scale tend to be increasing if the nonrival ideas are included as factors of production. These increasing returns conflict with perfect competition. Moreover, the compensation of nonrival old ideas in accordance with their current marginal cost of production—zero—will not provide the appropriate reward for the research effort that underlies the creation of new ideas.

Arrow (1962) and Sheshinski (1967) constructed models in which ideas were unintended by-products of production or investment, a mechanism described as learning by doing. In these models, each person's discoveries immediately spilled over to the entire economy, an instantaneous diffusion process that might be technically feasible because knowledge is nonrival. Romer (1986) showed later that the competitive framework can be retained in this case to determine an equilibrium rate of technological advance, but the resulting growth rate typically would not be Pareto optimal. More generally, the competitive framework breaks down if discoveries depend in part on purposive research and development (R&D) effort and if an individual's innovations spread only gradually to other producers. In this realistic setting, a decentralized theory of technological progress requires basic changes in the framework to incorporate elements of imperfect competition. These additions to the theory did not come until Romer's (1987, 1990) research in the late 1980s.

The initial wave of the new research—Romer (1986), Lucas (1988), and Rebelo (1991)—built on the work of Arrow (1962), Sheshinski (1967), and Uzawa (1965) and did not really introduce a theory of technological change. In these models, growth may go on indefinitely because the returns to investment in a broad class of capital goods, which includes human capital, do not necessarily diminish as economies develop. (This idea goes back to Knight 1944.) Spillovers of knowledge across producers and external benefits from human capital are parts of this process, but only because they help to avoid the tendency for diminishing returns to capital.

The incorporation of R&D theories and imperfect competition into the growth framework began with Romer (1987, 1990) and includes significant contributions by Aghion and Howitt (1992) and Grossman and Helpman (1991, chaps. 3, 4). Barro and Sala-i-Martin (1995, chaps. 6, 7) provide expositions and extensions of these models. In these settings, technological advance results from purposive R&D activity, and this activity is rewarded, along the lines of Schumpeter (1934), by some form of ex post monopoly power. If there is no tendency to run out of ideas, then growth rates can remain positive in the long run. The rate of growth and the underlying amount of inventive activity tend, however, not to be Pareto optimal because of distortions related to the creation of the new goods and methods of production. In these frameworks, the long-term growth rate depends on governmental actions, such as taxation, maintenance of law and order, provision of infrastructure services, protection of intellectual property rights, and regulation of international trade, financial markets, and other aspects of the economy. The government therefore has great potential for good or ill through its influence on the long-term rate of growth.

One shortcoming of the early versions of endogenous growth theories is that they no longer predicted conditional convergence. Since this behavior is a strong empirical regularity in the data for countries and regions, it was important to extend the new theories to restore the convergence property. One such extension involves the diffusion of technology (see Barro and Sala-i-Martin 1997). Whereas the analysis of discovery relates to the rate of technological progress in leading-edge economies, the study of diffusion pertains to the manner in which follower economies share by imitation in these advances. Since imitation tends to be cheaper than innovation, the diffusion models predict a form of conditional convergence that resembles the predictions of the neoclassical growth model. Therefore, this framework combines the long-run growth of the endogenous growth theories (from the discovery of ideas in the leading-edge economies) with the convergence behavior of the neoclassical growth model (from the gradual imitation by followers).

Endogenous growth theories that include the discovery of new ideas and methods of production are important for providing possible explanations for long-term growth. Yet the recent cross-country empirical work on growth has received more inspiration from the older, neoclassical model, as extended to include government policies, human capital, and the diffusion of technology. Theories of basic technological change seem most important for understanding why the world as a whole can continue to grow indefinitely in per capita terms. But these theories have less to do with the determination of relative rates of growth across countries, the key element studied in cross-country statistical analyses. The remainder of this chapter deals with the findings from this kind of cross-country empirical work.

Framework for the Analysis of Growth Across Countries

The framework for the determination of growth follows the extended version of the neoclassical model as already described. In equation form, the model can be represented as

$$Dy = f(y, y^*), \tag{1.1}$$

where Dy is the growth rate of per capita output, y is the current level of per capita output, and y^* is the long-run or steady-state level of per capita output.[1] The growth rate, Dy, is diminishing in y for given y^* and rising in y^* for given y. The target value y^* depends on an array of choice and environmental variables. The private sector's choices include saving rates, labor supply, and fertility rates, each of which depends on preferences and costs. The government's choices involve spending in various categories, tax rates, the extent of distortions of markets and business decisions, maintenance of the rule of law and property rights, and the degree of political freedom. Also relevant for an open economy is the terms of trade, typically given to a small country by external conditions.

For a given initial level of per capita output, y, an increase in the steady-state level, y^*, raises the per capita growth rate over a transition interval. For example, if the government improves the climate for business activity—say, by reducing burdens from regulation, corruption, and taxation or by enhancing property rights—the growth rate increases for awhile. Similar effects arise if people decide to have fewer children or (at least in a closed economy) to save a larger fraction of their incomes.

In these cases, the increase in the target, y^*, translates into a transitional increase in the economy's growth rate. As output, y, rises, the workings of diminishing returns eventually restore the growth rate, Dy, to a value determined by the rate of technological progress. Since the transitions tend to be lengthy, the growth effects from shifts in government policy or private behavior persist for a long time.

For given values of the choice and environmental variables—and, hence, y^*—a higher starting level of per capita output, y, implies a lower per capita growth rate. This effect corresponds to conditional convergence. Note, however, that poor countries would not grow rapidly on average if they tend also to have low steady-state positions, y^*. In fact, a low level of y^* explains why a country would typically have a low observed value of y in some arbitrarily chosen initial period.

The last result shows that the framework can be reconciled with the now familiar lack of correlation between the growth rate and initial level of real per capita GDP across a large number of countries over the period 1960 to 1990.

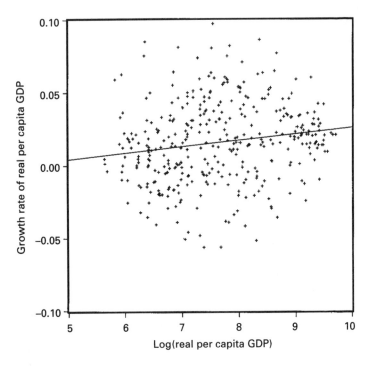

Figure 1.1
Simple correlation between growth and level of GDP

Figure 1.1 shows that this relationship is virtually nil.[2] (The slope actually has the wrong sign—slightly positive—but is not statistically significant.) The interpretation from the standpoint of the neoclassical model is that the initially poor countries, which show up closer to the origin along the horizontal axis, are not systematically far below their steady-state positions and therefore do not tend to grow relatively fast. The isolation of the convergence force requires a conditioning on the determinants of the steady state, as in the cross-country empirical analysis discussed in the next section.

Even if convergence held in an absolute sense—that is, if y^* were identical across economies and the poorer places thus tended to grow faster—the dispersion of per capita product would not necessarily narrow over time. The evolution of dispersion, or inequality, depends on a weighing of the convergence force against effects from the shocks that impinge on each economy. These shocks, if independent across economies, tend to create dispersion and therefore work against the equalizing pressure from convergence.

The idea that the tendency for the poor to grow faster than the rich implies a negative trend in inequality is a fallacy; in fact, it is Galton's fallacy, as discussed in the growth context by Quah (1993) and Hart (1995). Galton's (1886, 1889, chap. 7) research indicated that the deviation of children's heights (and other physical and mental characteristics) from the mean of the population was positively correlated with the parents' deviation, but the amount of deviation tended to regress—or converge—toward zero. Nevertheless, the population's distribution of heights did not tend systematically to narrow over time.

The explanation of these facts is that a measure of the population's dispersion—say, the standard deviation of the log of height (or GDP)—would tend to adjust toward a long-run value that depends on the rapidity of the reversion to the mean (the rate of convergence) and the variance of random shocks to height (or GDP). If the determinants of the long-run distribution do not change, then dispersion would tend to rise or fall depending on whether it happened to start below or above its long-run value. Moreover, if the underlying determinants stay constant for a long time, then the observed distribution for a large population would remain fixed (despite the presence of the convergence tendency).

Empirically, for 114 countries with data, the standard deviation of the log of real per capita GDP rose from 0.89 in 1960 to 1.14 in 1990. This observation of increased inequality does not reject the convergence implications of the neoclassical growth model, partly because the predicted convergence is only conditional and partly because the poor tending to grow faster than the rich is not the same as a declining trend in inequality.

Empirical Findings on Growth Across Countries

Table 1.1 shows results from regressions that use the general framework of equation 1.1. The regressions apply to a panel of roughly one hundred countries observed from 1960 to 1990.[3] The dependent variables are the growth rates of real per capita GDP over three periods: 1965–1975, 1975–1985, and 1985–1990.[4] (The first period begins in 1965 rather than 1960, so that the 1960 value of real per capita GDP can be used as an instrument.) Henceforth, the term GDP will be used as a shorthand to refer to real per capita GDP.

Table 1.1
Regressions for per capita growth rate

Independent variable	(1)	(2)
Log(GDP)	−.0254 (.0031)	−.0225 (.0032)
Male secondary and higher schooling	.0118 (.0025)	.0098 (.0025)
Log(life expectancy)	.0423 (.0137)	.0418 (.0139)
Log(GDP) ∗ male schooling	−.0062 (.0017)	−.0052 (.0017)
Log(fertility rate)	−.0161 (.0053)	−.0135 (.0053)
Government consumption ratio	−.136 (.026)	−.115 (.027)
Rule of law index	.0293 (.0054)	.0262 (.0055)
Terms of trade change	.137 (.030)	.127 (.030)
Democracy index	.090 [a] (.027)	.094 (.027)
Democracy index squared	−.088 (.024)	−.091 (.024)
Inflation rate	−.043 (.008)	−.039 (.008)
Sub-Saharan Africa dummy		−.0042 [b] (.0043)
Latin America dummy		−.0054 (.0032)
East Asia dummy		.0050 (.0041)
R^2	.58, .52, .42	.60, .52, .47
Number of observations	80, 87, 84	80, 87, 84

Table 1.1 (continued)

Notes: The system has three equations, where the dependent variables are the growth rate of real per capita GDP for 1965–1975, 1975–1985, and 1985–1990. The variables GDP (real per capita gross domestic product) and male schooling (years of attainment for the population aged twenty-five and over at the secondary and higher levels) refer to 1965, 1975, and 1985. Life expectancy at birth is for 1960–1964, 1970–1974, and 1980–1984. The variable log(GDP) ∗ male schooling is the product of log(GDP) (expressed as a deviation from the sample mean) and the male upper-level schooling variable (also expressed as a deviation from the sample mean). The rule of law index applies to the early 1980s (one observation for each country). The terms of trade variable is the growth rate over each period of the ratio of export to import prices. The inflation rate is the growth rate over each period of a consumer price index (or of the GDP deflator in a few cases). The other variables are measured as averages over each period. These variables are the log of the total fertility rate, the ratio of government consumption (exclusive of defense and education) to GDP, and the democracy index. Column 2 includes dummy variables for sub-Saharan Africa, Latin America, and East Asia. Individual constants (not shown) are also estimated for each period.

Estimation is by three-stage least-squares (with different instrumental variables used for each equation). The instruments include the five-year earlier value of log(GDP) (for example, for 1960 in the 1965–1975 equation); the actual values of the schooling, life expectancy, rule of law, and terms of trade variables; and, in column 2, the three area dummy variables. Additional instruments are earlier values of the other variables except the inflation rate. For example, the 1965–1975 equation uses the averages of the fertility rate and the government spending ratio for 1960–1964. Dummies for former colonies of Spain or Portugal and for former colonies of other countries aside from Britain and France are included as instruments. The instrument list also includes the cross product of the lagged value of log(GDP) (expressed as a deviation from the sample mean) with the male schooling variable (expressed as a deviation from the sample mean).

The estimation weights countries equally but allows for different error variances in each period and for correlation of these errors over time. The estimated correlation of the errors for column 1 is −0.13 between the 1965–1975 and 1975–1985 equations, 0.05 between the 1965–1975 and 1985–1990

Table 1.1 (continued)

(Notes, continued) equations, and 0.04 between the 1975–1985 and 1985–1990 equations. The pattern is similar for column 2. The estimates are virtually the same if the errors are assumed to be independent over the time periods. Standard errors of the coefficient estimates are shown in parentheses. The R^2 values and numbers of observations apply to each period individually.

[a] p value for joint significance of two democracy variables is 0.0006 in column 1 and 0.0004 in column 2.

[b] p value for joint significance of three dummy variables is 0.11.

Some previous analysis, such as Barro (1991), used a cross-sectional framework; that is, the growth rate and the explanatory variables were observed only once per country. The main reason to extend to a panel setup is to expand the sample information. Although the main evidence turns out to come from the cross-sectional (between-country) variation, the time-series (within-country) dimension provides some additional information. This information is greatest for variables that have varied a good deal over time within countries, such as the terms of trade and inflation.

The underlying theory relates to long-term growth, and the precise timing between growth and its determinants is not well specified at the high frequencies characteristic of business cycles. For example, relationships at the annual frequency would likely be dominated by mistiming and, hence, effectively by measurement error. In addition, many of the variables considered—such as fertility rates, life expectancy, and educational attainment—are not actually measured for many countries at periods finer than five or ten years. These considerations suggest a focus on the determination of growth rates over fairly long intervals. As a compromise with the quest for additional information, I settled on periods of five or ten years; specifically, growth rates were considered for 1965–1975 and 1975–1985 and for a final five-year period, 1985–1990. When the data through 1995 become available, the third period will be lengthened to 1985–1995.

The estimation uses an instrumental-variable technique, where some of the instruments are earlier values of the regressors. (The method is three-stage least squares, except that each equation contains a different set of instruments; see the notes to table 1.1 for details.) This approach may be satisfactory because the residuals from the growth rate equations are essentially uncorrelated across the periods. In any event, the regressions describe the relation between growth rates and prior values of the explanatory variables.

The regression shown in column 1 in table 1.1 includes explanatory variables that can be interpreted as initial values of state variables or as choice and environmental variables. The state variables include the initial level of GDP and measures of human capital in the forms of schooling and health. The GDP level reflects endowments of physical capital and natural resources (and also depends on effort and the unobserved level of technology). The choice and environmental variables are the fertility rate, government consumption spending, an index of the maintenance of the rule of law, the change in the terms of trade, an index of democracy (political rights), and the inflation rate. The roles of democracy and inflation will be discussed in the subsequent chapters.

Initial Level of GDP

For given values of the other explanatory variables, the neoclassical model predicts a negative coefficient on initial GDP, which enters in the system in logarithmic form.[5] The coefficient on the log of initial GDP has the interpretation of a conditional rate of convergence. If the other explanatory variables are held constant, then the economy tends to approach its long-run position at the rate indicated by the magnitude of the coefficient.[6] The estimated coefficient of -0.025 (s.e. $= 0.003$) is highly significant and implies a conditional rate of convergence of 2.5 percent per year.[7] The rate of convergence is slow in the sense that it would take the economy twenty-seven years to get halfway toward the steady-state level of output and eighty-nine years to get 90 percent of the way. Similarly slow rates of convergence have been found for regional data, such as the U.S. states, Canadian provinces, Japanese prefectures, and regions of the main Western European countries (see Barro and Sala-i-Martin 1995, chap. 11).

Figure 1.2 shows the partial relation between growth and the starting level of GDP, as implied by the regression from column 1 of table 1.1. The horizontal axis plots log(GDP) for 1965, 1975, and 1985 for the observations in the regression sample. The vertical axis shows the corresponding growth rate of GDP after filtering out the parts explained by all

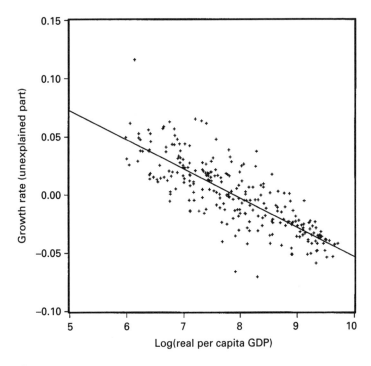

Figure 1.2
Growth rate versus level of GDP

explanatory variables other than log(GDP).[8] Thus, the negative slope shows the conditional convergence relation, that is, the effect of log(GDP) on the growth rate for given values of the other independent variables. In contrast to the lack of a simple correlation in figure 1.1, the conditional convergence relation in figure 1.2 is clearly defined in the graph. Also, the graph indicates that the relation is not driven by a few outliers and does not appear to be nonlinear.

Initial Level of Human Capital

Initial human capital appears in three variables in the system: average years of attainment for males aged twenty-five and over in secondary and higher schools at the start of each period, the log of life expectancy at birth at the start of each period (an indicator of health status),[9] and an interaction between the log of initial GDP and the years of male secondary and higher schooling. The data on years of schooling are updated and improved versions of the figures reported in Barro and Lee (1993).

The results show a significantly positive effect on growth from the years of schooling at the secondary and higher level for males aged twenty-five and over (0.0118 [0.0025]).[10] On impact, an extra year of male upper-level schooling is therefore estimated to raise the growth rate by a substantial 1.2 percentage points per year. (In 1990, the mean of the schooling variable was 1.9 years, with a standard deviation of 1.3 years.) The partial relation between the growth rate and the schooling variable—constructed analogously to the method described for log(GDP) in note 8—is shown in figure 1.3.

Male primary schooling (of persons aged twenty-five and over) has an insignificant effect if added to the system—the estimated coefficient is −0.0005 (0.0011)—whereas that on upper-level schooling remains similar to that found before (0.0119 [0.0025]). Thus, growth is predicted by male schooling at the upper levels but not at the primary level. Primary

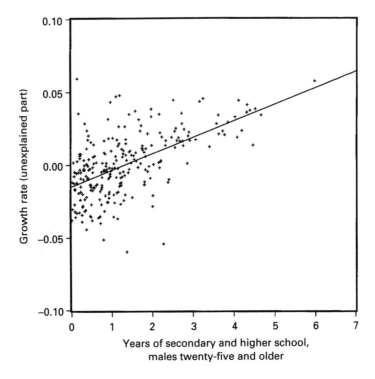

Figure 1.3
Growth rate versus male schooling

schooling, nevertheless, is indirectly growth enhancing because it is a prerequisite for training at the secondary and higher levels.

More surprising, female education at various levels is not significantly related to subsequent growth. For example, if years of schooling at the secondary and higher levels for females aged twenty-five and over is added to the system

shown in column 1 of table 1.1, then the estimated coefficient of this variable is −0.0023 (0.0046), whereas that for
males remains significantly positive at 0.0132 (0.0036). For
primary schooling of women aged twenty-five and over,
the estimated coefficient is −0.0001 (0.0012), whereas that
for men (twenty-five and over for secondary and higher
schools) is 0.0118 (0.0025). Thus, these findings do not support the hypothesis that education of women is a key to
economic growth.[11]

Some additional results indicate that female schooling is important for other indicators of economic development, such
as fertility, infant mortality, and political freedom (see the
next chapter). Specifically, female primary education has a
strong negative relation with the fertility rate (see Schultz
1989, Behrman 1990, and Barro and Lee 1994). A reasonable
inference from this relation is that female education would
spur economic growth by lowering fertility, and this effect
is not captured in the regressions shown in table 1.1 because
the fertility rate is already held constant. If the fertility rate
is omitted from the system, then the estimated coefficient on
female primary schooling (the level of female schooling that
affects fertility inversely) is 0.0012 (0.0012), which is positive but not significantly different from zero. Thus, there
is only slight evidence that female education enhances economic growth through this indirect channel.

Returning to column 1 of table 1.1, the significantly negative estimated coefficient of the interaction term between
male schooling and log(GDP), −0.0062 (0.0017), implies that

more years of school raise the sensitivity of growth to the starting level of GDP. Starting from a position at the sample mean, an extra year of male upper-level schooling is estimated to raise the magnitude of the convergence coefficient from 0.026 to 0.032. This result supports theories that stress the positive effect of education on an economy's ability to absorb new technologies. The partial relation between the growth rate and the interaction variable appears in figure 1.4. (The points at the far right of the diagram are for the most developed countries, such as the United States, Canada, and Sweden, which have high values of GDP and schooling.)

The regression in column 1 of table 1.1 also reveals a significantly positive effect on growth from initial human capital in the form of health. The coefficient on the log of life expectancy is 0.042 (0.014). As an interpretation, it may be that life expectancy proxies not only for health status but more broadly for the quality of human capital. The partial relation between growth and life expectancy is shown in figure 1.5.

Fertility Rate

If the population is growing, then a portion of the economy's investment is used to provide capital for new workers rather than to raise capital per worker. For this reason, a higher rate of population growth has a negative effect on y^*, the steady-state level of output per effective worker in

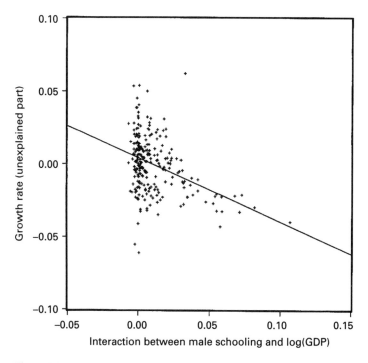

Figure 1.4
Growth rate versus interaction between schooling and level of GDP

the neoclassical growth model. A reinforcing effect is that a higher fertility rate means that increased resources must be devoted to child rearing rather than to production of goods (see Becker and Barro 1988). The regression in column 1 of table 1.1 shows a significantly negative coefficient, -0.016 (0.005), on the log of the total fertility rate. The partial relation between growth and fertility is in figure 1.6.

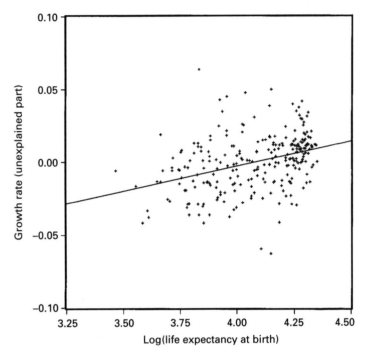

Figure 1.5
Growth rate versus life expectancy

Fertility decisions are surely endogenous; previous research has shown that fertility typically declines with measures of prosperity, especially female primary education (see Schultz 1989, Behrman 1990, and Barro and Lee 1994). The estimated coefficient of the fertility rate in the growth regression shows the response to higher fertility for given values of male schooling, life expectancy, GDP, and so on. Since the average of the fertility rate over the preceding five years

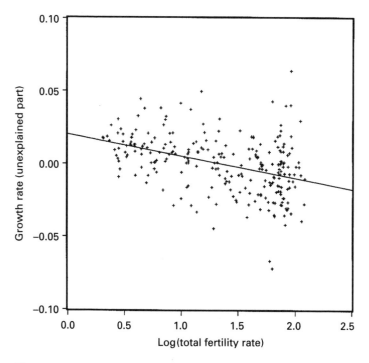

Figure 1.6
Growth rate versus fertility rate

is used as an instrument, the coefficient likely reflects the impact of fertility on growth, rather than vice versa. (In any event, the reverse effect would involve the level of GDP rather than its growth rate.) Thus, although population growth cannot be characterized as the most important element in economic progress, the results do suggest that an exogenous drop in birthrates would raise the growth rate of per capita output.

Government Consumption

The regression in column 1 of table 1.1 shows a significantly negative effect on growth from the ratio of government consumption (measured exclusive of spending on education and defense) to GDP. The estimated coefficient is −0.136 (0.026). (The period average of the ratio enters into the regression, and the average of the ratio over the previous five years is used as an instrument.) The particular measure of government spending is intended to approximate the outlays that do not improve productivity. Hence, the conclusion is that a greater volume of nonproductive government spending—and the associated taxation—reduces the growth rate for a given starting value of GDP. In this sense, big government is bad for growth. The partial relation between growth and the government consumption variable appears in figure 1.7.

The Rule of Law Index

Knack and Keefer (1995) discuss a variety of subjective country indexes prepared for fee-paying international investors and distributed as the *International Country Risk Guide*. (The various time series cover 1982 to 1995 and are available from Political Risk Services of Syracuse, New York.) The concepts covered include quality of the bureaucracy, political corruption, likelihood of government repudiation of contracts, risk of government expropriation, and overall maintenance of the rule of law. The general idea is

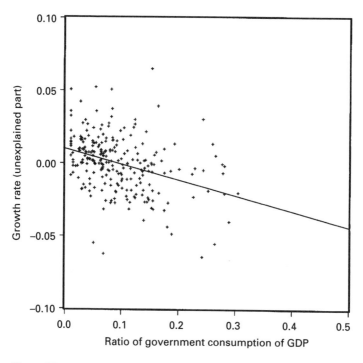

Figure 1.7
Growth rate versus government consumption ratio

to gauge the attractiveness of a country's investment climate by considering the effectiveness of law enforcement, the sanctity of contracts, and the state of other influences on the security of property rights. Although these data are subjective, they have the virtue of being prepared contemporaneously by local experts. Moreover, the willingness of customers to pay substantial fees for this information is perhaps some testament to their validity.

Among the various series available, the indicator for overall maintenance of the rule of law seemed a priori to be most relevant for investment and growth. This indicator was initially measured in seven categories on a 0 to 6 scale, with 6 the most favorable. The scale has been revised here to 0 to 1, with 0 indicating the worst maintenance of the rule of law and 1 the best.

The rule of law variable (observed, because of lack of earlier data, only once for each country in the early 1980s) was included in the regression system reported in column 1 of table 1.1 and has a significantly positive coefficient, 0.0293 (0.0054). (The other measures of investment risk, including political corruption and various indicators of political instability, are insignificant in these kinds of growth regressions if the rule of law index is also included.) The interpretation is that greater maintenance of the rule of law is favorable to growth. Specifically, an improvement by one rank in the underlying index (corresponding to a rise by 0.167 in the rule of law variable) is estimated to raise the growth rate on impact by 0.5 percentage point. The partial relation between growth and the rule of law index is in figure 1.8. (Note that only seven values for the index are observed.)

Terms of Trade

Changes in the terms of trade have often been stressed as important influences on developing countries, which typically specialize their exports in a few primary products. The

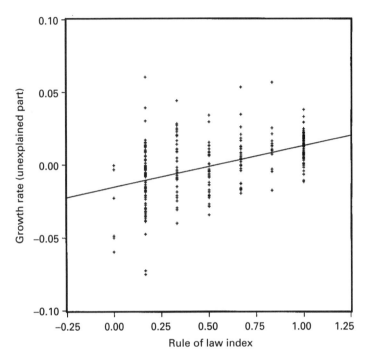

Figure 1.8
Growth rate versus rule of law index

effect of a change in the terms of trade, measured as the ratio of export to import prices, on GDP is, however, not mechanical. If the physical quantities of goods produced domestically do not change, then an improvement in the terms of trade raises real domestic income and probably consumption but would not affect real GDP. Movements in real GDP occur only if the shift in the terms of trade stimulates a change in domestic employment and output. For example, an oil-importing country might react to an increase in the relative price of oil by cutting back on its employment and production.

The result in column 1 of table 1.1 shows a significantly positive coefficient on the terms of trade: 0.14 (0.03). (The change in the terms of trade is regarded as exogenous to an individual country's growth rate and is therefore included as an instrument.) Thus, an improvement in the terms of trade apparently does stimulate an expansion of domestic output. The partial relation with growth appears in figure 1.9. Although the terms of trade variable is statistically significant, it turns out not to be the key element in the weak growth performance of many poor countries, such as those in sub-Saharan Africa.

Regional Variables

It has often been observed that recent rates of economic growth have been surprisingly low in sub-Saharan Africa and Latin America and surprisingly high in East Asia. For 1975–1985, the mean per capita growth rate for all 124 countries with data was 1.0 percent, compared with −0.3 percent in 43 sub-Saharan African countries, −0.1 percent in 24 Latin American countries, and 3.7 percent in 12 East Asian countries. For 1985–1990, the average growth rate was again 1.0 percent (for 129 places), compared with 0.1 percent in 40 sub-Saharan African countries, 0.4 percent in 29 Latin American countries, and 4.0 percent in 15 East Asian countries. An important question is whether these regions

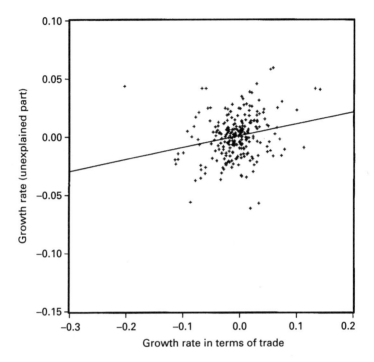

Figure 1.9
Growth rate versus change in terms of trade

continue to look like outliers once the explanatory variables considered in table 1.1 have been taken into account.

In some previous cross-country regression studies, such as Barro (1991), dummy variables for sub-Saharan Africa and Latin America were found to enter negatively and significantly into growth regressions. However, column 2 of table 1.1 shows that dummies for these two areas and also for East Asia are individually insignificant. (The p value for joint significance of the three dummy variables is 0.11.) Thus, the unusual growth experiences of these three regions are mostly accounted for by the explanatory variables.

The inclusion of the inflation rate is critical for eliminating the significance of the Latin America dummy (this interaction is discussed in the next chapter). The Latin America dummy also becomes significant if the fertility rate or the government consumption ratio is omitted. In the case of sub-Saharan Africa, the government consumption ratio is the only individual variable whose omission causes the dummy to become significant. For East Asia, the dummy is significant if male schooling, the rule of law indicator, or the democracy variables are deleted.

Investment Ratio

In the neoclassical growth model for a closed economy, the saving rate is exogenous and equal to the ratio of investment to output. A higher saving rate raises the steady-state level of output per effective worker and thereby raises the growth rate for a given starting value of GDP. Some empirical studies of cross-country growth have also reported an important positive role for the investment ratio (see, for example, DeLong and Summers 1991 and Mankiw, Romer, and Weil 1992).

Reverse causation is, however, likely to be important here. A positive coefficient on the contemporaneous investment ratio in a growth regression may reflect the positive relation between growth opportunities and investment rather than the positive effect of an exogenously higher investment ratio on the growth rate. This reverse effect is especially likely to apply for open economies. Even if cross-country differences in saving ratios are exogenous with respect to growth, the decision to invest domestically rather than abroad would reflect the domestic prospects for returns on investment, which would relate to the domestic opportunities for growth.

The system from column 1 of table 1.1 has been expanded to include the period-average investment ratio as an explanatory variable. If the instrument list includes the investment ratio over the previous five years but not the contemporaneous value, then the estimated coefficient on the investment variable is positive but not statistically significant: 0.027 (0.021). In contrast, the estimated coefficient is almost twice as high and statistically significant if the contemporaneous investment ratio is included as an instrument: 0.043 (0.018). These findings suggest that much of the positive estimated effect of the investment ratio on growth in typical cross-country regressions reflects the reverse relation between growth prospects and investment. Blömstrom, Lipsey, and Zejan (1993) reach similar conclusions in their study of investment and growth.

To interpret these results further, table 1.2 shows regression systems in which the dependent variables are the average ratios of investment to GDP for 1965–1974, 1975–1984, and 1985–1989. The independent variables (aside from the

Table 1.2
Regressions for investment ratio

Independent variable	(1)	(2)
Log(GDP)	−.010 (.011)	−.005 (.011)
Male secondary and higher schooling	−.0032 (.0088)	−.0064 (.0085)
Log(life expectancy)	.259 (.050)	.274 (.051)
Log(GDP) ∗ male schooling	−.0004 (.0057)	.0009 (.0055)
Log(fertility rate)	−.0028 (.0192)	.0056 (.0186)
Government consumption ratio	−.264 (.089)	−.216 (.087)
Rule of law index	.092 (.023)	.074 (.024)
Terms of trade change	.074 (.068)	.070 (.064)
Democracy index	.148 (.069)	.168 (.070)
Democracy index squared	−.142 (.061)	−.153 (.062)
Inflation rate	−.053 (.022)	−.036 (.021)
Sub-Saharan Africa dummy		−.013[a] (.019)
Latin America dummy		−.038 (.014)
East Asia dummy		.010 (.017)
R^2	.59, .62, .61	.60, .65, .67
Number of observations	80, 87, 84	80, 87, 84

Table 1.2 (continued)

Notes: The systems correspond to those described in table 1.1, except that the dependent variables are now the average ratios of real investment (private plus public) to real GDP over the periods 1965–1974, 1975–1984, and 1985–1989. The correlation of the errors across the equations is substantial in the systems for investment. For example, for column 1, the correlation between the first and second periods is 0.53, that between the first and third periods is 0.35, and that between the second and third periods is 0.62.

[a] p value for joint significance of three dummy variables is 0.03.

investment ratio) are the same as those used in table 1.1. The key finding in column 1 of table 1.2 is that a number of the variables that are found to enhance the growth rate in table 1.1 also appear as stimulants to investment. In particular, the investment ratio is positively related to life expectancy (a proxy for the quality of human capital) and the rule of law index and negatively related to the government consumption ratio and the inflation rate. The investment ratio also follows the same sort of quadratic relation with democracy that showed up for the growth rate. The effects of democracy are explored in the next chapter.

A reasonable interpretation of the results is that some policy variables—such as better maintenance of the rule of law, lower government consumption, and price stability—encourage economic growth partly by stimulating investment. However, if investment is higher for given values of the policy instruments—perhaps because of variations in thriftiness across economies that lack perfect capital mobility—then the positive effect on growth is weak, as indicated by the estimated coefficient of 0.027 (0.021) on the investment ratio.

Cross-Country Regressions and Country Fixed Effects

A comparison of figures 1.1 and 1.2 shows that it is critical
to hold fixed the determinants of the long-run target value,
y^*, in equation 1.1 to isolate the conditional convergence
force—that is, the effect of initial GDP, y, on the growth rate,
Dy, for a given y^*. Since y and y^* tend to be positively correlated, the estimated coefficient on y would be biased upward if y^* were not held constant. Since the true coefficient
on y is negative, the omission of y^* tends to generate an
underestimate of the rate of convergence, possibly even to
the extent of estimating divergence (a positive coefficient on
y) rather than convergence. Hence, the omission of y^* can
account for the incorrect (positive) sign in the simple relation between Dy and y shown in figure 1.1.

One remaining problem in figure 1.2 is that the estimated
rate of convergence would still tend to be underestimated
if the measures used to hold fixed y^* were imperfect (as
they must be). Specifically, underestimation of the convergence rate would tend to apply if the omitted determinants
of y^* were still positively correlated with y after holding
fixed the variables included to measure y^*. It is hard to get
a direct assessment of the magnitude of this problem, although the isolation of y^*—like variables that have a lot of
explanatory power for growth—as highlighted in the previous discussion—should lessen the error.

Some researchers prefer to handle this type of estimation
problem by allowing for an unobserved fixed effect for each

country (see Knight, Loayza, and Villanueva 1993; Islam 1995; and Caselli, Esquivel, and Lefort 1996). Usually this treatment is applied by first differencing all variables in order to eliminate the fixed effect. This procedure works if the underlying determinants of y^*, such as government policies and preferences about saving and fertility, do not vary over time within a country. In practice, problems would still exist because unobserved shifts in y^* could still be correlated with the movements in y.

The main drawback of the fixed-effects technique is that it relies on time-series information within countries; that is, it eliminates the cross-sectional information, which is the principal strength of the broad cross-country data. Aside from losing information and, hence, precision, first differencing of the data tends to emphasize measurement error over signal. In particular, the estimation becomes more sensitive to incorrect timing in the relation between growth and its determinants.

If first differences of the determinants of y^* are retained in the estimation, then measurement error tends to bias toward zero the estimated coefficients of these variables. For the estimated coefficient of Dy on y, one should consider a regression of y (log[GDP]) on its own lag. Measurement error tends to bias this value toward zero and leads accordingly to an overestimate of the rate of convergence.

Column 1 of table 1.3 shows the results from estimation of a first-differenced version of the system from column 1 of

Table 1.3
Results from first differences and a cross-section

Independent variable	(1) First difference	(2) Cross-section	(3) Panel	(4) p value
Log(GDP)	−.0444 (.0066)	−.0220 (.0041)	−.0242 (.0028)	.000
Male schooling	−.0032 (.0045)	.0141 (.0030)	.0123 (.0023)	.68
Log(life expectancy)	−.0820 (.0381)	.0172 (.0184)	.0388 (.0124)	.002
Log(GDP) ∗ male schooling	.0052 (.0035)	−.0077 (.0019)	−.0070 (.0015)	.18
Log(fertility rate)	−.0396 (.0116)	−.0206 (.0066)	−.0156 (.0049)	.11
Government consumption ratio	.000 (.048)	−.114 (.026)	−.110 (.021)	.024
Rule of law index		.0294 (.0066)	.0300 (.0051)	
Terms of trade change	.102 (.027)	.078 (.078)	.129 (.029)	.92
Democracy index	.019 (.029)	.071 (.026)	.048 (.019)	.51
Democracy index squared	−.014 (.026)	−.074 (.023)	−.051 (.016)	.28
Inflation rate	−.032 (.005)	−.030 (.006)	−.028 (.004)	.12
R^2	.29, .44	.76	.56, .53, .49	
Number of observations	88, 91	80	83, 88, 84	

Notes: The systems are variants of the one shown in column 1 of table 1.1. Column 1 uses first differences of all variables and is estimated by the seemingly unrelated (SUR) technique, which allows for a different error variance for the two periods and correlation of the errors across the

Table 1.3 (continued)

(Notes, continued) periods. Column 2 uses means of all variables and is estimated by ordinary least squares (OLS). Column 3 is the same as column 1 of table 1.1, except that estimation is by SUR rather than three-stage least squares. The p values in column 4 refer to Wald tests of equality of the coefficients from columns 1 and 2.

table 1.1. This setup includes two equations. In the first, the dependent variable is the growth rate of GDP from 1975 to 1985, less that from 1965 to 1975. In the second, the dependent variable is the growth rate from 1985 to 1990, less that from 1975 to 1985. Similarly, the independent variables are first differences of the variables that appear in column 1 of table 1.1, for example, the first equation contains log(GDP) for 1975 less log(GDP) for 1965. The system is estimated in a seemingly unrelated (SUR) framework, which allows for correlation of the errors across the two equations. (Since the residuals from the growth rate equations in table 1.1 were essentially uncorrelated across the time periods, the residuals for the two equations in column 1 of table 1.3 have a strong negative correlation.)

Column 2 of table 1.3 shows the results from ordinary least squares (OLS) estimation of a pure cross-section, which contains one observation for each country. In this case, the dependent and independent variables are means over the three time periods of the variables used in column 1 of table 1.1.

Finally, column 3 of table 1.3 is the same as column 1 of table 1.1, except that the estimation is by the SUR technique instead of instrumental variables. This setup is basically a weighted combination of the time-series information from column 1 of table 1.3 with the cross-sectional information from column 2 of the table. In the main, these estimates are close to those shown in column 1 of table 1.1. The principal differences from the use of instruments show up in the estimated coefficients of the democracy and inflation variables.

If one compares the estimated coefficients from the first-difference specification with those from the cross section, then the biggest discrepancy is in the estimated convergence rate: -0.044 (0.007) in column 1 versus -0.022 (0.004) in column 2. The hypothesis of equality for these coefficients is rejected by a Wald test with a p value of 0.000 (see column 4 of the table). For the other independent variables, the only cases in which the estimated coefficients from the two specifications differ significantly at the 5 percent level (when variables are considered one at a time) are those for life expectancy and government consumption. However, a joint test of equality for all ten pairs of coefficients rejects decisively.

The standard errors of the coefficients in columns 1 and 2 indicate the information available from the time-series and cross-sectional dimensions of the panel data. For many of the variables—log(GDP), male schooling, log(life expectancy), the interaction between log(GDP) and male schooling, log(fertility rate), and the government consumption ratio—the standard errors are much smaller in column 2 than in column 1. This pattern indicates that the cross-country (between) variation in these independent variables is much more informative than the time-series (within-country) variation. The extreme situation is for the rule of law variable, which has no time-series dimension (as currently measured) and therefore effectively has an infinite standard error in the first-difference form. The only case in which the standard error is noticeably smaller in column 1 is for the terms of trade; the variations here relate more to changes over time than to differences across countries. For democracy and inflation, the standard errors are similar in the two contexts.

Many researchers seem to prefer the results from variants of first-difference specifications, as in column 1 of table 1.3, because of their concern with the possible bias from correlated fixed effects. The high estimated convergence coefficient from this column—4.4 percent per year—is similar to that reported from more sophisticated but related techniques by Knight, Loayza, and Villanueva (1993, p. 529), Islam (1995, tables 3, 4); and Caselli, Esquivel, and Lefort (1996, tables 3, 4). However, the higher magnitude of these convergence coefficients, relative to those found from the panel estimation in column 3 of table 1.3 or column 1 of table 1.1, may reflect an increase in the relative amount of measurement error from the exclusion of the cross-sectional information. That is, instead of eliminating the fixed-effects bias (which tends to underestimate the convergence rate), the first-difference procedure may mainly exaggerate the measurement error bias (which tends to overestimate the convergence rate).

The results in column 1 also show that it is hard to isolate effects from the explanatory variables other than lagged GDP in a pure time-series context. The only estimated coefficients that are significant at the 5 percent critical level are those for the fertility rate, the terms of trade, and the inflation rate. Life expectancy is marginally significant with the wrong sign. One reason for these findings is that the time series offers little variation in many of the variables. In addition, the model likely misspecifies the timing between growth and its determinants, and this error is much more important for time-series estimation than in a cross section.

Undoubtedly the confidence in the results would be greater if the estimated coefficients from first-difference and cross-sectional forms did not differ significantly. Improvements in specification—for example, with regard to the lag structure between growth and its determinants—may produce more uniform results, but at this stage, there seems to be no basis for preferring the first-difference estimates to the cross-sectional ones. I have focused on panel results—column 3 of table 1.3 or column 1 of table 1.1—as a weighing of these two imperfect sources of information, where the weights are determined (by means of the SUR or three-stage least-squares procedures) from the relative informativeness of the two sources.

Growth Projections

The results from column 1 of table 1.1 can be used to construct long-term forecasts of economic growth for individual countries. These predictions have been constructed by using recent observations of the explanatory variables: GDP in 1994 (or sometimes earlier), schooling in 1990, life expectancy and fertility in 1993, consumer price index (CPI) inflation through 1993 or 1994, the rule of law indicator for 1995, the democracy index for 1994, and government consumption in the late 1980s.[12] Table 1.4 shows the twenty predicted best and worst performers from 1996 to 2000 out of the eighty-six countries that have the necessary data to make these projections.[13] There is, however, a substantial margin of error (as much as two percentage points) in the prediction for an individual country.

For all eighty-six countries, the average forecast of per capita growth is 2.4 percent per year. The breakdown by region is 3.7 percent for 18 Asian countries, 2.9 percent for twenty-two Latin American countries, 2.4 percent for twenty-one Organization for Economic Cooperation and Development (OECD) countries (not including Japan, Turkey, and Mexico), and 0.5 percent for eighteen sub-Saharan African countries.

It is no surprise that many old and new tigers of East Asia are forecasted to grow rapidly; South Korea, Malaysia, Singapore, Thailand, Hong Kong, and Taiwan are on the high-growth list. (Japan falls short with 3.2 percent growth.) The unexpected finding is the presence in the high-growth group of Asian laggards of the past: the Philippines, India, Sri Lanka, and Pakistan. (China and Vietnam would likely also appear but are excluded because of missing data.)

Table 1.4
Winners and losers for prospective economic growth

Top 20 prospects		Bottom 20 prospects	
Country	Predicted growth rate of real per capita GDP 1996–2000 (% per year)	Country	Predicted growth rate of real per capita GDP 1996–2000 (% per year)
South Korea	6.2	Sierra Leone	−3.6
Philippines	5.6	Sudan	−2.7
Dominican Republic	5.4	Malawi	−0.2
		Bangladesh	−0.2
India	5.3	Niger	−0.1
Poland	5.2	Zaire	−0.1
Peru	5.2	Gambia	0.1
Sri Lanka	5.0	Botswana	0.1
Malaysia	5.0	Senegal	0.2
Argentina	4.7	Papua New Guinea	0.2
Singapore	4.6		
Thailand	4.6	Brazil	0.2
Greece	4.6	Congo	0.3
Chile	4.3	Algeria	0.3
Paraguay	4.2	Zambia	0.5
Hong Kong	4.2	Mali	0.8
Guyana	4.2	Nicaragua	0.8
Pakistan	3.9	Cameroon	1.1
Taiwan	3.8	Trinidad	1.2
Ecuador	3.8	Costa Rica	1.3
Egypt	3.8	Uganda	1.3

Regional patterns:

All countries (86)	2.4
Sub-Saharan Africa (18)	0.5
Latin America (22)	2.9
Asia (18)	3.7
OECD (21)	2.4

South Korea places at the top with 6.2 percent growth because it has high educational attainment, strong rule of law, low government spending, low fertility, high investment, and low inflation. Although their underlying growth determinants are less favorable, the Philippines, India, and Sri Lanka place nearly as high in projected growth rates because their levels of per capita GDP are only one-eighth to one-quarter as large as South Korea's. These are cases in which the convergence force generates rapid growth.

The high-growth list also has substantial representation in South America: Peru, Argentina, Chile, Paraguay, Guyana, and Ecuador. A key assumption here is that the recently achieved macroeconomic stability, as reflected in relatively low inflation rates, will be maintained. As a contrast, Brazil appears on the low-growth list with roughly zero per capita growth. Aside from low school attainment, a major element is projected inflation of around 50 percent.

In Central Europe, posttransformation Poland appears as a prospective fast grower, and Hungary (with 3.5 percent projected growth) just misses the list. Other countries, such as the Czech Republic, would likely have appeared but are excluded because of lack of data.

On the low-growth list, thirteen of the twenty countries are in sub-Saharan Africa. (Other countries, such as Nigeria, Rwanda, and Somalia, would likely have been included if not for their missing data.) Sierra Leone, as a prototype, has weak rule of law, low school attainment, high fertility, low life expectancy, no political freedom, high government consumption, moderately high inflation, and virtually no investment. Being poor, which Sierra Leone and the other African countries surely are, is not enough to generate high growth.

Among OECD countries, the only place on the high-growth list is Greece. (Spain comes close with 3.8 percent growth.) Many of the advanced economies nearly made the low-growth list: Denmark at 1.3 percent, Norway at 1.4 percent, the United States at 1.4 percent, Sweden at 1.7 percent, Finland at 1.9 percent, the United Kingdom at 2.0 percent, Canada at 2.0 percent, Germany at 2.1 percent, Italy at 2.2 percent, and France at 2.4 percent. (Note that the growth rate of the level of GDP adds the growth rate of population—roughly 1 percent per year for the United States and smaller amounts in Western Europe.)

One can also use the results to ask, somewhat more speculatively, whether some changes in institutions or policies could move the United States, the United Kingdom, or another advanced country to the high-growth list, that is, raise the long-term per capita growth rate from $1\frac{1}{2}$ to 2 percent to around 4 percent. Unfortunately, the answer seems to be no. The institutions and policies in the advanced countries are already reasonably good (despite possible excesses of transfer programs and regulations), and long-term per capita growth much above 2 percent seems to be incompatible with the prosperity that has already been attained.

It would probably be feasible to raise the long-term growth rate by a few tenths of a percentage point by cutting tax rates and nonproductive government spending or by eliminating harmful regulations. (Some of these variables may be important but could not be measured in the cross-country empirical work discussed above.) Moreover, increases in growth rates by a few tenths of a percentage point matter a lot in the long run and are surely worth the trouble. On the negative side, it would be possible to lower the growth rate by a few tenths of a percentage point by moving away from price stability or interfering further with free markets. There is no evidence that increases in infrastructure investment, research subsidies, or educational spending would help a lot. Basically, 2 percent per capita growth seems to be about as good as it gets in the long run for a country that is already rich.

2   The Interplay between Economic and Political Development

Theoretical Notions

Economic freedoms, in the form of free markets and small governments that focus on the maintenance of property rights, are often thought to encourage economic growth. This view receives support from the empirical findings discussed in chapter 1. The connection between political and economic freedom is more controversial, as stressed in the theoretical parts of the recent surveys by Sirowy and Inkeles (1990) and Przeworski and Limongi (1993). Some observers, such as Friedman (1962), believe that the two freedoms are mutually reinforcing. In this view, an expansion of political rights—more "democracy"—fosters economic rights and tends thereby to stimulate growth. But the growth-retarding aspects of democracy have also been stressed. These features involve the tendency to enact rich-to-poor redistributions of income (including land reforms) in systems of majority voting and the possibly enhanced role of interest groups in systems with representative legislatures.

Authoritarian regimes may partially avoid these drawbacks of democracy. Moreover, nothing in principle prevents non-democratic governments from maintaining economic freedoms and private property. A dictator does not have to engage in central planning. Examples of autocracies that have expanded economic freedoms include the Pinochet government in Chile, the Fujimori administration in Peru, the shah's regime in Iran, and several previous and current governments in East Asia. Furthermore, as Schwarz (1992) observes, most OECD countries began their modern economic development in systems with limited political rights and became full-fledged representative democracies only much later.

The effects of autocracy on growth are adverse, however, if a dictator uses his or her power to steal the nation's wealth and to carry out nonproductive investments. Many governments in Africa, some in Latin America, some in the formerly planned economies of Eastern Europe, and the Marcos administration in the Philippines seem to fit this pattern. Thus, history suggests that dictators come in two types: one whose personal objectives often conflict with growth promotion and another whose interests dictate a preoccupation with economic development. This perspective accords with Sah's (1991, pp. 70–71) view that dictatorship is a form of risky investment. In any event, the theory that determines which kind of dictatorship will prevail seems to be missing.

Democratic institutions provide a check on governmental power and thereby limit the potential of public officials to amass personal wealth and carry out unpopular policies. Since at least some policies that stimulate growth will also be politically popular, more political rights tend to be growth enhancing on this count. Thus, the net effect of democracy on growth is theoretically inconclusive.

The interplay between political institutions and economic outcomes also involves the effect of the standard of living on a country's propensity to experience democracy. A common view since Lipset's (1959) research is that prosperity stimulates democracy, an idea often described as the Lipset hypothesis. Lipset (1959, p. 75) apparently prefers to view it as the Aristotle hypothesis: "From Aristotle down to the present, men have argued that only in a wealthy society in which relatively few citizens lived in real poverty could a situation exist in which the mass of the population could intelligently participate in politics and could develop the self-restraint necessary to avoid succumbing to the appeals of irresponsible demagogues." (For a statement of Aristotle's views, see Aristotle 1932, book VI.)

Theoretical models of the effect of prosperity on democracy are not well developed. Lipset (1959, pp. 83–84) emphasizes increased education and an enlarged middle class as elements that expand "receptivity to democratic political tolerance norms" (a phrase that I wish I understood). He also stresses Tocqueville's (1835) idea that private organizations and institutions are important as checks on dictatorship. This point has been extended by Putnam (1993), who argues that the propensity for civic activity is the key underpinning of good government in the regions of Italy.[1] For Huber, Rueschemeyer, and Stephens (1993, pp. 74–75), the crucial concept is that capitalist development lowers the power of the landlord class and raises the power and ability to organize of the working and middle classes.

Despite the lack of a compelling underlying theory, the cross-country evidence examined in this study confirms that the Lipset hypothesis is a strong empirical regularity. In particular, increases in various measures of the standard of living tend to generate a gradual rise in democracy. In contrast, democracies that arise without prior economic development—sometimes because they are imposed by former colonial powers or international organizations—tend not to last. Given the strength of this empirical regularity, one would think that clear-cut theoretical analyses ought to be attainable. (This seems to be a case where the analysis works in practice but not in theory.)

Effects of Democracy on Economic Growth

The principal measure of democracy used in this study is the indicator of political rights compiled by Gastil and his associates (1982–1983 and subsequent issues) from 1972 to 1994. A related variable from Bollen (1990) is used for 1960 and 1965.[2] The Gastil concept of political rights is indicated by his basic definition: "Political rights are rights to participate meaningfully in the political process. In a democracy this means the right of all adults to vote and compete for public office, and for elected representatives to have a decisive vote on public policies" (Gastil, 1986–1987 ed., p. 7). In addition to the basic definition, the classification scheme rates countries (somewhat impressionistically) as less democratic if minority parties have little influence on policy.

Gastil applied the concept of political rights on a subjective basis to classify countries annually into seven categories, where group 1 is the highest level of political rights and group 7 is the lowest. The classification is made by Gastil and his associates based on an array of published and unpublished information about each country. Unlike the rule of law index, discussed in chapter 1, the subjective ranking is not made directly by local observers.

The original ranking from 1 to 7 has been converted here to a scale from 0 to 1, where 0 corresponds to the fewest political rights (Gastil's rank 7) and 1 to the most political rights (Gastil's rank 1). The scale from 0 to 1 corresponds to the system used by Bollen.

Figure 2.1 shows the time path of the unweighted average across countries of the democracy index for 1960, 1965, and 1972–1994. The number of countries covered rises from 99 in 1960 to 109 in 1965 and 138 from 1972 to 1994. The figure

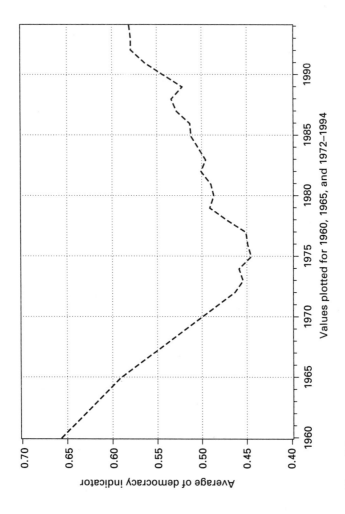

Figure 2.1
Democracy in the world

shows that the mean of the democracy index peaked at 0.66 in 1960, fell to a low point of 0.44 in 1975, and rose subsequently to 0.58 in 1994.

Figures 2.2 and 2.3 demonstrate that the main source of the decline in democracy after 1960 is the experience in sub-Saharan Africa. Figure 2.2 shows that the average of the democracy indicator in sub-Saharan Africa peaked at 0.58 in 1960 (twenty-six countries), then (for forty-three countries) fell to low points of 0.19 in 1977 and 0.18 in 1989 before rising to 0.38 in 1994. This pattern emerges because many of the African countries began with democratic institutions when they became independent in the early 1960s, but most evolved into one-party dictatorships by the early 1970s. (See Bollen 1990 for further discussion.) The democratization in Africa since 1989 has been substantial; whether it will be sustained is not yet known.

For countries outside sub-Saharan Africa, Figure 2.3 shows that the average of the democracy index fell from 0.68 in 1960 (seventy-three countries) to 0.55 in 1975 (ninety-five countries). It then returned to 0.69 in 1990 but fell to 0.67 in 1994.

Some of the analysis also uses the Gastil indicator of civil liberties. The definition here is that "civil liberties are rights to free expression, to organize or demonstrate, as well as rights to a degree of autonomy such as is provided by freedom of religion, education, travel, and other personal

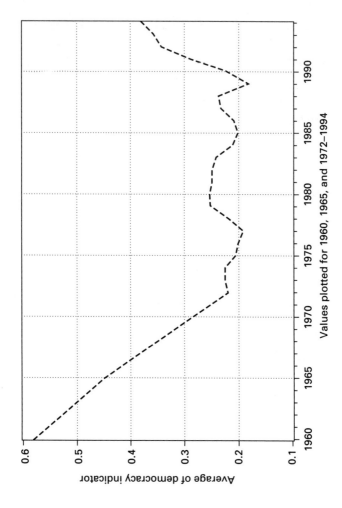

Figure 2.2
Democracy in sub-Saharan Africa

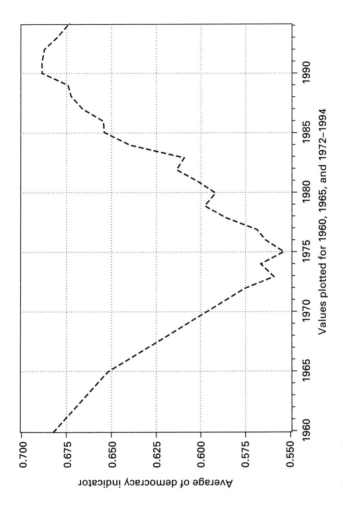

Figure 2.3
Democracy outside sub-Saharan Africa

rights" (Gastil 1986–1987 ed., p. 7). Otherwise the subjective approach is the same as the one used for the political rights indicator. The original scale for the civil liberties index from 1 to 7 has again been converted to 0 to 1, where 0 represents the fewest civil liberties and 1 the most. In practice, as observed by Inkeles (1991), the indicator for civil liberties turns out to be extremely highly correlated with that for political rights.

The previous discussion indicated that the net effect of more political freedom on growth is theoretically ambiguous. If the indicator for democracy is entered linearly into the regression system of table 1.1, then the resulting coefficient estimate turns out to be negative but statistically insignificant: −0.003 (0.006).[3]

The system shown in column 1 of table 1.1 allows for a quadratic in the indicator. In this case, the estimated coefficients on democracy and its square are each statistically significant. (The p value for joint significance of the two terms is 0.001.) The pattern of results—a positive coefficient on the linear term and a negative coefficient on the square—means that growth is increasing in democracy at low levels of democracy, but the relation turns negative once a moderate amount of political freedom has been attained.[4] The estimated turning point occurs at an indicator value of approximately 0.5, which corresponds to the levels of democracy in 1994 for Malaysia and Mexico.

Table 1.2 shows that an analogous nonlinear relation shows up in the effect of democracy on the investment ratio. The level of democracy that maximizes this ratio is again around 0.5.

One way to interpret the results is that in the worst dictatorships, an increase in political rights tends to increase growth and investment because the benefit from limitations on governmental power is the key matter. But in places that have already achieved a moderate amount of democracy, a further increase in political rights impairs growth and investment because the dominant effect comes from the intensified concern with income redistribution. Thus, growth would likely be reduced by further democratization beyond the levels attained in 1994 in countries such as Malaysia and Mexico. Moreover, political liberalization has probably gone beyond the point of growth maximization in places such as Chile, South Korea, and Taiwan. (These countries went from levels for the democracy indicator of 0.17, 0.33, and 0.33, respectively, in the early 1980s to 0.83, 0.83, and 0.67, respectively, in 1994.)

Figure 2.4 shows the partial relation between the growth rate and democracy indicator, as implied by the system shown in column 1 of table 1.1. (The concentration of points at a democracy value of 1.0 corresponds to the many OECD countries that are rated as fully democratic.) An inverse U shape can be discerned in the plot, with many of the low- and high-democracy places exhibiting negative residuals.[5]

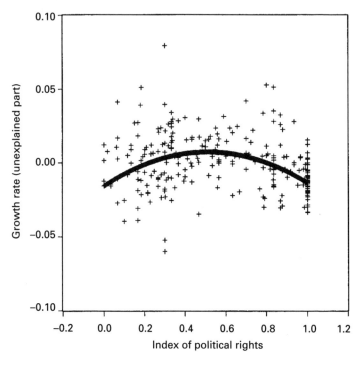

Figure 2.4
Growth rate versus indicator of democracy

Only a few of the observations with middle levels of democracy, such as Guyana over 1975–1985 and Pakistan over 1965–1975, have substantially negative residuals.

The overall relation between growth and democracy is far from perfect; for example, a number of countries with little democracy have large positive residuals. Also, the places with middle levels of democracy seem to avoid low growth rates but not to have especially high growth rates. Thus, there is only the suggestion of a nonlinear relation in which more democracy raises growth when political freedoms are weak but depresses growth when a moderate amount of freedom is already established. One cannot conclude from this evidence that more or less democracy is a critical element for economic growth.

Framework for the Determination of Democracy

Inspection of the cross-country data suggests that countries at low levels of economic development typically do not sustain democracy. For example, the political freedoms installed in most of the newly independent African states in the early 1960s did not tend to last. Conversely, nondemocratic places that experience substantial economic development tend to become more democratic. Examples are Chile, South Korea, Taiwan, Spain, and Portugal. Moreover, the countries of Central and Eastern Europe, which have been reasonably advanced economically for some time, especially in terms of education, eventually became more democratic. Thus, a casual view of the data tends to confirm the Lipset hypothesis.

To assess this hypothesis formally, I consider a system of the form

$$DEMOC_{it} = a_0 + a_1 Z_{i,t-T} + a_2 DEMOC_{i,t-T} + u_{it}, \qquad (2.1)$$

where i is the country, t is the time period, and T is a time lag, usually taken to be five years. *DEMOC* is the indicator for democracy; Z is a vector of variables, such as per capita GDP and education, that influence the extent of democracy; and u is an error term. The idea in the equation is that if $0 < a_2 < 1$, then the extent of democracy in a country converges gradually over time toward a (moving) target that is determined by the Z variables. In practice, the Z variables are themselves highly persistent over time.

Operationally I use a panel setup in which the dependent variable, $DEMOC_{it}$, is observed at most six times for each country: 1972, 1975, 1980, 1985, 1990, and 1994. (The year 1972 is the initial date of the Gastil sample.) The variables $Z_{i,t-T}$ and $DEMOC_{i,t-T}$ refer to variables observed roughly five years prior to these dates.[6] (The values for $DEMOC_{t-T}$ are for 1965, 1972, 1975, and so on.)

Regression Results for Democracy

The basic regression results are in column 1 of table 2.1. This system contains a single constant term and the five-year lag value of democracy.[7] The explanatory variables also include several indicators of the level of the standard of living: the log of real per capita GDP, the log of life expectancy at birth,[8] and measures of educational attainment. These indicators are observed roughly five years prior to the dependent variable. The schooling figures that turn out to have the most explanatory power are the years of attainment at the primary level for males and females aged fifteen and over.

A dummy for oil-exporting countries, as designated by the International Monetary Fund (IMF),[9] is also included as a rough adjustment of GDP for the contribution of natural resources. That is, the income generated from natural resources such as oil may create less pressure for democratization than income associated with the accumulation of human and physical capital.

The specification includes some other possible influences on democracy that have been proposed in the political science literature that began with Lipset (1959) (see Lipset, Seong, and Torres 1993 and Lipset 1994 for discussion). The urbanization rate is often mentioned as a determinant of democracy, although the sign of this influence is not clear on theoretical grounds. (The easier communication and transportation in urban areas may make it easier for the populace to resist oppression, but these forces also make it easier for a dictator to monitor and control his or her subjects.) The simple correlation between democracy and urbanization is strongly positive, but urbanization is also positively related to real per capita GDP and the other measures of the standard of living that are included as regressors. In any event, the system includes the rate of urbanization observed five years prior to the dependent variable.[10]

The system also includes a measure of country size, the log of the five-year-earlier level of population. It is, how-

Table 2.1
Regressions for democracy and civil liberties indexes

	Dependent variables		
	(1)	(2)	(3)
Independent variable	Democracy	Democracy	Civil liberties
Constant	−0.91 (0.26)	−0.54 (0.28)	−0.48 (0.21)
$DEMOC_{t-5}$	0.672 (0.028)	0.650 (0.042)	0.680 (0.026)
Log(GDP)	0.045 (0.017)	0.041 (0.019)	0.037 (0.014)
Male primary schooling	−0.056 (0.014)	−0.047 (0.015)	−0.037 (0.011)
Female primary schooling	0.060 (0.014)	0.053 (0.015)	0.047 (0.011)
Log(life expectancy)	0.187 (0.076)	0.100 (0.085)	0.096 (0.062)
Urbanization rate	−0.102 (0.048)	−0.061 (0.051)	−0.032 (0.039)
Log(population)	0.0061 (0.0043)	0.0049 (0.0046)	−0.0016 (0.0035)
Oil country dummy	−0.107 (0.030)	−0.129 (0.032)	−0.101 (0.025)
$DEMOC_{t-10}$		0.035 (0.040)	
R^2	.59, .74, .66, .74, .76, .55	.73, .67, .75, .76, .57	.59, .81, .77, .83, .70, .72
Number of observations	85, 97, 101, 102, 105, 102	89, 101, 102, 105, 102	85, 97, 101, 102, 105, 102

Notes: System 1 has six equations, where the dependent variables are the values of the Gastil democracy index for 1972, 1975, 1980, 1985, 1990, and 1994. The variable $DEMOC_{t-5}$ is for 1965, 1972, and so on. (The data for

Table 2.1 (continued)

(Notes, continued) 1965 are from Bollen 1990.) The variables GDP (real per capita GDP), male and female primary schooling (years of attainment for persons aged fifteen and over at the primary level), urbanization rate, and population refer to 1965, 1970, and so on. Life expectancy at birth applies to 1960–1964, 1965–1969, and so on. The oil dummy equals 1 for countries designated as oil exporting by the International Monetary Fund (IMF) and 0 otherwise. System 2 contains only the five equations that start with the 1975 value of the democracy index. This system adds a second lag of the index (applying to 1965, 1972, etc.) as an explanatory variable. System 3 is the same as system 1 except that the dependent variable and its lag are for the Gastil civil liberties index. (The value for 1965, from Bollen 1990, coincides with the democracy index.)

Each system contains only one constant, as shown. The estimation, by the SUR technique, weights countries equally but allows for different error variances in each period and for correlation of these errors over the periods. Standard errors of the estimated coefficients are shown in parentheses. The R^2 values apply to each period individually.

ever, not apparent a priori whether a larger place is more or less likely to be democratic. (One selection problem here is that the existing countries had not become too large to split apart. See Alesina and Spolaore 1995 for a discussion of the determinants of country size.)

The first observation from column 1 of table 2.1 is that the estimated coefficient on lagged democracy is 0.67 (s.e. = 0.03). Thus, democracy is highly persistent over time, but roughly one-third of the adjustment to a target position (determined by the other variables) occurs over five years.

The results for the standard of living are broadly highly supportive of the Lipset idea that more prosperous places are more likely to be democratic. The estimated coefficients on log(GDP) and log(life expectancy) are each significantly positive: 0.046 (0.017) and 0.19 (0.08), respectively. Thus, the target level of democracy is increasing in these indicators of the standard of living.

The estimated coefficient on years of primary school attainment for females aged fifteen and over is significantly positive, 0.060 (0.014), whereas that for male schooling is significantly negative: −0.056 (0.014).[11] A surprising aspect of this result is that once GDP and life expectancy are held constant, the level of schooling does not help to explain democracy. However, a smaller excess of male over female attainment—that is, more equal educational opportunity across the sexes—raises the target level of democracy. The gap between male and female attainment may be viewed as a proxy for the equality of schooling more generally. However, an explicit measure of educational inequality does not have a lot of explanatory power for democracy. Perhaps more promising is the idea, reminiscent of Tocqueville (1835), that expanded educational opportunity for women goes along with a social structure that is generally more participatory and, hence, more receptive to democracy.

The oil country dummy is significantly negative, −0.11 (0.03), thereby indicating that the high level of per capita GDP in oil countries does not have the usual positive effect on democratization. It seems plausible that this result would extend to natural resource activities more generally. To test this idea, I introduced the measures of natural resource intensity used by Sachs and Warner (1995): the ratios (in

1971) of primary product exports to total exports or to GDP. However, these variables are insignificant if added to the system shown in column 1 of table 2.1; for example, the estimated coefficient on the primary product share of exports is 0.005 (0.029). The estimated coefficient on the oil dummy is then −0.113 (0.032), about the same as that shown in table 2.1. It seems likely, however, that a better measure of natural resources would outperform the oil dummy.

The p value for the joint significance of the variables that measure the standard of living—log(GDP), log(life expectancy), male and female primary schooling, and the oil dummy—is 0.000. Thus, the general link between democracy and the standard of living is firmly established.[12]

The urbanization rate enters negatively in the system shown in column 1 of table 2.1; the estimated coefficient is −0.10 (0.05). Thus, once the indicators of the standard of living are held constant, it is not true that more rural places are less likely to be democratic.

The coefficient on the log of population is positive but not significant: 0.006 (0.004). (The simple correlation between democracy and country size is also close to zero.) Thus, there is no clear evidence on whether larger countries are more or less likely to be democratic.

Column 2 of table 2.1 adds a second lag of democracy, that is, a value applying roughly ten years prior to the dependent variable. (This system includes only the five equations that begin with the observation of democracy for 1975.) The estimated coefficients on the five- and ten-year lags are 0.65 (0.04) and 0.04 (0.04), respectively. Hence, there is no indication that the longer-term history of democracy matters once the situation five years previously is held constant.

Table 2.2 considers some other possible determinants of democracy, many of which have been proposed in the political science literature. These additional variables are entered one set at a time into the six-period regression system described in column 1 of table 2.1. For example, on the first line of table 2.2, the infant mortality rate has an estimated coefficient of −0.42 (0.53) and is therefore insignificant. Infant mortality and life expectancy are highly correlated and are essentially indistinguishable in the regressions.

The second regression in table 2.2 adds years of school attainment for males and females aged fifteen and over at the secondary and higher levels. These values are individually and jointly insignificant, whereas the estimated coefficients on primary attainment remain significant (−0.064 [0.017] for males and 0.069 [0.017] for females). Hence, it appears to be early education that matters for democratization. Similar results apply to the determination of fertility rates and health status. However, rates of economic growth (and investment) relate far more to secondary and higher schooling than to primary education.

Regression 3 of table 2.2 includes a measure of inequality, as gauged by Gini coefficients for data on income distribution. (A higher Gini coefficient signifies more inequality.) Figures for the early 1960s are used in the first three equations (for 1972, 1975, and 1980), and values for the early 1980s are used in the last three equations (for 1985, 1990, and 1994). These data on income distribution have been used in numerous studies but are thought to be highly inaccurate.[13] In any event, the estimated coefficient on inequality is essentially zero. Although the sample of observations is much reduced (because of the limited data on inequality), the estimated coefficients of the other explanatory variables remain similar to those shown in column 1 of table 2.1.

The finding that inequality is unimportant for democracy may reflect the poor quality of the data on income distribution rather than the irrelevance of inequality for democracy. In particular, the other independent variables—especially female primary schooling—may be superior to the reported Gini coefficients as measures of income inequality. The data on educational attainment at seven levels allow us to construct measures of schooling inequality. Regression 4 of table 2.2 uses as an independent variable the standard deviation of log (1+ years of schooling)[14] for the population of both sexes aged fifteen and over. This variable is observed for 1965, 1970, and so on. The estimated coefficient is negative (-0.058 [0.043]), indicating that more inequality of schooling goes along with less democracy, but statistically insignificant at conventional critical levels. The estimated coefficients of male and female primary schooling remain significant here: -0.047 (0.015) and 0.051 (0.016), respectively. If the Gini coefficient for years of schooling is used as an alternative measure of educational inequality, then the

Table 2.2
Additional determinants of democracy

Independent variables	Regression coefficients
1. Infant mortality rate	−0.42 (0.53)
2. Male upper schooling	0.021 (0.024)
Female upper schooling	−0.016 (0.027)
	p value = 0.60
3. Income inequality (Gini coefficient)	0.02 (0.12)
4. Educational inequality (standard deviation of log[1+years of schooling] for population aged fifteen and over)	−0.058 (0.043)
5. Ethnolinguistic fractionalization	−0.004 (0.032)
6. Rule of law index	0.048 (0.056)
7. Dummy for former colony	−0.010 (0.017)
8. Dummy for British colony	−0.018 (0.018)
Dummy for French colony	−0.007 (0.026)
Dummy for Spanish colony	−0.002 (0.022)
Dummy for Portuguese colony	0.031 (0.044)
Dummy for other colony	−0.010 (0.032)
	p value = 0.82
9. Muslim religion fraction	−0.076 (0.028)
Protestant religion fraction	0.054 (0.031)
Hindu religion fraction	0.119 (0.052)
Buddhist religion fraction	0.046 (0.054)
Miscellaneous Eastern religion fraction	−0.130 (0.073)
Jewish religion fraction	0.058 (0.076)
Nonreligion fraction	−0.266 (0.096)
Other religion fraction	−0.061 (0.052)
	p value = 0.0002

Notes: The indicated groups of explanatory variables are added, one at a time, to the system for the democracy index shown in column 1 of table 2.1.

Table 2.2 (continued)

(Notes, continued) (Case 6 applies only to the three periods that start with the value of the democracy index for 1985.)

The infant mortality rate applies to 1965, 1970, and so on. Upper schooling is the years of secondary and higher schooling for males or females aged fifteen and over. Income inequality is the Gini coefficient for income data applying around 1960 in the first three equations and in the early 1980s in the last three equations. A higher number indicates more inequality. Educational inequality is the standard deviation of log(1+years of schooling) for the overall population aged fifteen and over in 1965, 1970, etc. The ethnolinguistic fractionalization variable, which runs between 0 and 1, is a measure of heterogeneity of language and ethnicity. The number, observed once for each country, represents the probability that two randomly selected persons will come from different groups; hence, a higher value signifies more heterogeneity. See Mauro (1995) for a discussion of these data. The rule of law index, discussed by Knack and Keefer (1995) and available for 1982–1995 from Political Risk Services, is a subjective indicator of the extent of maintenance of the rule of law. The variable runs from 0 to 1, with a higher value indicating a more favorable environment.

Colony is a dummy for countries that are former or present colonies, where any country that was independent before 1776 is designated as a noncolony. In case 8, dummies for former British, French, Spanish, Portuguese, and other colonies are added together to the system from column 1 of table 2.1. Colonial status is based on the most recent ruler; for example, the Philippines is attributed to the United States rather than Spain.

In case 9, the fractions of the population affiliated with eight major religious groups are entered together into the system from column 1 of table 2.1. The left-out religion category is Catholic. The religion data are for 1970 (in the first three equations) and 1980 (in the last three equations) and come from Barrett (1982). The Protestant group includes Anglicans, Eastern Orthodox, marginal Protestants (Jehovah's Witnesses, Mormons, new age cults), and cryto-Christians (secret believers in Christ not professing publicly). Eastern religions include Chinese folk religions, Confucianism, and new religions. The nonreligion category comprises those professing no religion and atheism. Other religions include Parsis, Spiritists, tribal religions, indigenous Third World Christians not of Western importation, and Bahais. Jains and Sikhs are classed with Hindus.

estimated coefficient is again negative but even less statistically significant. Hence, these results indicate that male
and female years of schooling do not enter the regressions
merely as proxies for educational inequality.

The population's degree of heterogeneity with respect to
ethnicity, language, and culture may also matter for democracy. The usual idea is that more heterogeneity makes it
more difficult to sustain democracy. A standard measure of
a population's heterogeneity is its ethnolinguistic fractionalization, a measure of disparity of languages and ethnicity within a country. (See Mauro 1995 for a discussion.) The
variable runs between 0 and 1 and is intended to measure
the probability that two randomly chosen persons in a country will come from different groups. Hence, 0 is the most ho-
mogeneous and 1 is the most heterogeneous. Regression 5
of table 2.2 shows that the estimated coefficient of the fractionalization variable (observed once per country) is close to
zero.

A measure of the rule of law has substantial explanatory
power for economic growth. However, the connection between political freedom and the rule of law is unclear, as
stressed in the theoretical parts of the recent surveys by
Sirowy and Inkeles (1990) and Przeworski and Limongi
(1993). Some observers, such as Friedman (1962), argue that
the two variables are mutually reinforcing, but others regard them as essentially independent.

Regression 6 of table 2.2 checks out this relationship by en-
tering lagged values of the rule of law index into the equa-

tions for democracy. Since the data on the rule of law begin in 1982, this system includes only the equations for democracy for 1985, 1990, and 1994. The values for the rule of law in this system apply to 1982, 1985, and 1990. The result is that the estimated coefficient on the rule of law variable is positive but insignificant, 0.048 (0.056). Thus, holding fixed the measures of standard of living, there is not much evidence that rule of law promotes political freedom. Less directly, however, an expansion of the rule of law would raise economic growth and lead over time to a higher standard of living and, hence, to more democracy.

The rule of law measure can also be viewed as the dependent variable in a system where the independent variables are own lags and lags of the other variables, including the democracy index. (Three equations—for 1985, 1990, and 1995—are used here.) In this setting, democracy turns out to enter with a positive coefficient, 0.026 (0.027), which is not significant at conventional critical levels. Thus, there is also not strong evidence that political freedom stimulates the maintenance of the rule of law.

Colonial heritage would be important for democracy if countries inherit tendencies for more or less political freedom from their previous rulers. For example, Lipset, Seong, and Torres (1993, p. 168) argue that British rule provided a crucial learning experience for subsequent democracy. In table 2.3, a noncolony is defined to be a country that was independent prior to and since 1775 (so that the United States is treated as a former colony of Britain). Each former colony is attributed to its most recent occupier; for example,

Table 2.3
Democracy in relation to colonial status and religion

	Number of countries	Democracy indicator (average 1975–1994)
Colonial status		
Noncolony	32	0.69
Colony	106	0.46
British colony	53	0.54
French colony	23	0.25
Spanish colony	16	0.60
Portuguese colony	5	0.28
Other colony	9	0.35
All countries	138	0.51
Religious affiliation		
Primary religious affiliation, 1980		
Catholic	49	0.60
Muslim	32	0.26
Protestant	24	0.78
Hindu	5	0.66
Buddhist	4	0.56
Miscellaneous Eastern religions	3	0.45
Jewish	1	0.85
Nonreligious	1	0.10
Other religion	17	0.28
All countries with data on religion	136	0.51

Note: See the discussion in the text and table 2.2 for definitions of colonial status and religious affiliation. Section II shows averages for 1975–1994 of the democracy measure for groups of countries in which the most common religious affiliation in 1980 is of the indicated type.

the Philippines is associated with the United States rather than Spain, Rwanda and Burundi are attached to Belgium rather than Germany, and several Caribbean countries are related to Britain rather than Spain. The classification treats as noncolonies places such as South Korea, Taiwan, Hungary, and Poland, which were occupied by a foreign power for some periods.

The first section of table 2.3 shows that the thirty-two non-colonies are more likely to be democratic (average value for the democracy indicator from 1975 to 1994 of 0.69) than are the colonies (average value of 0.46). Within the colonies, the former possessions of Britain and Spain are substantially more democratic than are those of France, Portugal, or other countries. (The former possessions of Spain would look less democratic in earlier periods.)

In the statistical analysis, with the measures of standard of living held constant, regression 7 of table 2.2 shows that a dummy variable for colonial status (1 for former colony, 0 for noncolony) is insignificant for democracy. Moreover, regression 8 indicates that a breakdown among British, French, Spanish, Portuguese, and other colonies fails to generate any significant coefficients. (The p value for joint significance of the five coefficients is 0.82.) These results, in conjunction with table 2.3, suggest that the influence of former colonial status on democratic tendency must work indirectly through effects on the standard of living, as measured here by GDP, life expectancy, and male and female primary schooling. These indirect links with colonial history are worth further study.

Religious affiliation has also been stressed as an important determinant of democracy (see Huntington 1991, pp. 71–85, and Lipset 1994, p. 5). (The theory of the interplay between religion and political structure is even less developed than are other aspects of the theory of democracy.) To check for a connection between religion and political freedom, I use data compiled by Jong-Wha Lee on the fractions of a country's population in 1970 and 1980 affiliated with nine major groups:[15] Catholic, Muslim, Protestant (including Anglican and some other Christian groups), Hindu (including Jains and Sikhs), Buddhist, miscellaneous Eastern religions (Chinese folk religions, Shinto, Confucianism, and new religionists), Jewish, no professed religion (including atheists), and other religious groups (such as Parsis, Bahais, Spiritists, tribal religions, and indigenous Third World Christians).

The second section of table 2.3 verifies that differences in a country's primary religious affiliation relate strongly to democracy. When countries are sorted in accordance with the most popular religion in 1980, the average of the democracy indicator from 1975 to 1994 is 0.85 for Jewish (1 country), 0.78 for Protestant (24 countries), 0.66 for Hindu (5 countries), 0.60 for Catholic (49 countries), 0.56 for Buddhist (4 countries), 0.45 for miscellaneous Eastern religions (3 countries), 0.28 for other religions (17 countries), and 0.26 for Muslim (32 countries). China is the only place in which nonreligion is the most common affiliation, and the average of the democracy index in this case is 0.10. The mean value of democracy for all 136 countries with data on religion is 0.51.

A prominent aspect of this breakdown is that Protestant countries are nearly always highly democratic, whereas Muslim countries are usually not democratic. Only 4 of the 32 Muslim countries have democracy indicators that averaged at least 0.5 for 1975–1994: Gambia, Senegal, Malaysia, and Turkey.

Regression 9 of table 2.2 shows the results when eight religious affiliation variables are entered into the equations for democracy.[16] (The omitted characteristic is chosen arbitrarily to be Catholic, the most prevalent religion when countries are weighted equally.) The regressions indicate that the only significant religion coefficients at the 5 percent critical level are for nonreligion, −0.27 (0.10); Hindu, 0.12 (0.05); and Muslim, −0.08 (0.03). The estimated coefficient for Protestant is positive but not significant, 0.05 (0.03). Thus, the strong explanatory power for religion that appears in table 2.3, especially the contrast in democratic tendency between Protestant and Muslim countries, is mostly reflected in the measures of standard of living, which are being held constant.

The p value of 0.0002 indicates that the eight religion coefficients are significant overall; however, much of this significance hinges on the presence of a few outlier countries.

For example, the significantly positive coefficient on Hindu mainly indicates that India and Mauritius are surprisingly democratic, given their indicators of the standard of living. If these two places are omitted from the sample, the estimated coefficient on Hindu falls to 0.041 (0.064). The significantly negative coefficient on nonreligion depends on the inclusion of China, the one country for which this affiliation exceeds 0.5.[17] If China is omitted, the estimated coefficient of nonreligion becomes −0.25 (0.14); that is, the point estimate is about the same, but the rise in the standard error eliminates the statistical significance.

The weak results on the estimated religion coefficients do not necessarily mean that religion is unimportant for understanding political freedom (or in other respects). Rather, the indication is that the main effects on democracy work indirectly through influences on the economic variables— for example, through effects on female schooling. Given the striking patterns that emerge in table 2.3, these channels are worth further investigation.

The democracy indicator is a narrow measure that focuses on political rights, specifically the role of elections. In contrast, the Gastil index of civil liberties is a broader concept that covers freedoms of speech, press, and religion and also considers a variety of legal protections. In practice, however, the civil liberties variable is highly correlated with the democracy index: 0.86 in 1972, 0.93 in 1980, 0.94 in 1990, and 0.91 in 1994. Given this high degree of correlation, it is not surprising that results with the civil liberties index as the dependent variable, shown in column 3 of table 2.1, look similar to those found for the democracy index.[18] This result suggests that the economic and social forces that promote political rights are similar to those that stimulate civil liberties.

Long-Run Forecasts of Democracy

The estimated relation from column 1 of table 2.1 implies a gradual adjustment of democracy toward the values determined by the explanatory variables aside from lagged democracy.[19] In a full system, the dynamics of these explanatory variables would also be determined. In practice, the levels of GDP and the other variables are highly persistent over time, although they evolve gradually in line with the process of economic development, some of which has already been studied in chapter 1 in terms of rates of economic growth.[20]

One simple way to relate the current level of democracy to its long-run target is to compute at each date the estimated level of democracy that would arise asymptotically if all the right-hand-side variables (aside from lagged democracy) were held fixed at their current values. For example, in 1975, the long-run level of democracy is calculated from the 1970 values (1965–1969 for life expectancy) of the regressors included in column 1 of table 2.1.[21] The resulting projected values for 1975 and 1994 are shown along with the actual values of democracy in table 2.4. The gap is the difference

Table 2.4
Actual and long-run values of democracy

Country	Democracy, 1975			Democracy, 1994		
	Actual	Projected	Gap	Actual	Projected	Gap
Algeria	0.17	0.01	0.16	0.00	0.20	−0.20
Benin	0.00	0.36	**−0.36**	0.83	0.24	**0.59**
Botswana	0.83	0.51	0.32	0.83	0.76	0.08
Cameroon	0.17	0.27	−0.10	0.17	0.38	−0.21
Central African Republic	0.00	0.15	−0.15	0.67	0.13	**0.54**
Congo	0.33			0.50	0.48	0.02
Egypt	0.17	0.38 [a]	−0.21	0.17	0.44	−0.27
Gambia	0.83	0.18 [a]	**0.65**	0.00	0.17	−0.17
Ghana	0.00	0.25	−0.25	0.33	0.21	0.12
Guinea-Bissau	0.17			0.67	0.18	**0.48**
Kenya	0.33	0.23	0.10	0.17	0.38	−0.21
Lesotho	0.33	0.59	−0.25	0.50	0.76	−0.26
Liberia	0.17	0.25	−0.08	0.00		
Malawi	0.00	0.06	−0.06	0.83	0.21	**0.63**
Mali	0.00	0.17	−0.17	0.83	0.27	**0.56**
Mauritius	0.83	0.48	**0.35**	1.00	0.75	0.25
Mozambique	0.17	0.33	−0.16	0.67	0.32	**0.34**
Niger	0.00	0.27	−0.27	0.67	0.32	**0.34**
Rwanda	0.00	0.31	−0.31	0.00	0.30	−0.30
Senegal	0.17	0.22	−0.05	0.50	0.28	0.22
Sierra Leone	0.17	0.18	−0.01	0.00	0.16	−0.16
South Africa	0.50	0.64	−0.14	0.83	0.61	0.23
Sudan	0.17	0.33	−0.16	0.00	0.39	**−0.39**
Swaziland	0.17	0.45	−0.29	0.17	0.54	**−0.37**
Tanzania	0.17	0.21	−0.05	0.17	0.26	−0.10
Togo	0.00	0.21	−0.21	0.17	0.15	0.01
Tunisia	0.17	0.35	−0.19	0.17	0.36	−0.19
Uganda	0.00	0.27	−0.27	0.33	0.32	0.02
Zaire	0.00	0.15	−0.15	0.00	0.07	−0.07
Zambia	0.33	0.15	0.18	0.67	0.07	**0.60**

Table 2.4 (continued)

Country	Democracy, 1975			Democracy, 1994		
	Actual	Projected	Gap	Actual	Projected	Gap
Zimbabwe	0.17	0.41	−0.24	0.33	0.48	−0.14
Barbados	1.00	0.84	0.16	1.00	0.92	0.08
Canada	1.00	0.96	0.04	1.00	(1.06)	−0.06
Costa Rica	1.00	0.76	0.24	1.00	0.86	0.14
Dominican Republic	0.50	0.57	−0.07	0.50	0.66	−0.16
El Salvador	0.83	0.46	**0.37**	0.67	0.63	0.03
Guatemala	0.50	0.50	0.00	0.50	0.63	−0.13
Haiti	0.17	0.36	−0.19	0.33	0.21	0.13
Honduras	0.17	0.49	−0.32	0.67	0.45	0.22
Jamaica	1.00	0.78	0.22	0.83	0.81	0.03
Mexico	0.50	0.56	−0.06	0.50	0.80	−0.30
Nicaragua	0.33	0.53	−0.19	0.50	0.56	−0.06
Panama	0.00	0.74	**−0.74**	0.83	0.79	0.04
Trinidad and Tobago	0.83	0.85	−0.02	1.00	0.88	0.12
United States	1.00	(1.02)	−0.02	1.00	(1.11)	−0.11
Argentina	0.50	0.74	−0.24	0.83	0.76	0.07
Bolivia	0.17	0.25	−0.09	0.83	0.45	**0.39**
Brazil	0.50	0.64	−0.14	0.83	0.76	0.08
Chile	0.00	0.65	**−0.65**	0.83	0.74	0.09
Colombia	0.83	0.59	0.25	0.67	0.83	−0.16
Ecuador	0.00	0.59	**−0.59**	0.83	0.72	0.11
Guyana	0.50	0.67	−0.17	0.83	0.65	0.19
Paraguay	0.33	0.61	−0.27	0.50	0.68	−0.18
Peru	0.17	0.41	−0.25	0.33	0.55	−0.21
Uruguay	0.33	0.75	**−0.41**	0.83	0.77	0.07
Venezuela	0.83	0.53	0.30	0.67	0.46	0.21
Bahrain	0.17			0.17	0.43	−0.27
Bangladesh	0.00	0.38	**−0.38**	0.83	0.46	**0.37**
China	0.00	0.53 [a]	**−0.53**	0.00	0.53	**−0.53**
Hong Kong	0.67	0.45	0.22	0.33	0.85	**−0.51**

Table 2.4 (continued)

Country	Democracy, 1975			Democracy, 1994		
	Actual	Projected	Gap	Actual	Projected	Gap
India	0.83	0.20	**0.63**	0.50	0.38	0.12
Indonesia	0.33	(–0.05)	**0.38**	0.00	0.25	–0.25
Iran	0.17	0.22	–0.05	0.17	0.26	–0.10
Iraq	0.00	0.15	–0.15	0.00	0.09	–0.09
Israel	0.83	0.71	0.12	1.00	0.86	0.14
Japan	0.83	0.91	–0.08	0.83	(1.06)	–0.23
Jordan	0.17	0.22	–0.06	0.50	0.57	–0.07
South Korea	0.33	0.50	–0.17	0.83	0.81	0.03
Malaysia	0.67	0.40	0.27	0.50	0.73	–0.23
Nepal	0.17	0.34	–0.17	0.67	0.33	**0.34**
Pakistan	0.33	0.30	0.03	0.67	0.44	0.23
Philippines	0.33	0.62	–0.29	0.67	0.74	–0.07
Singapore	0.33	0.36	–0.03	0.33	0.73	**–0.39**
Sri Lanka	0.83	0.70	0.13	0.50	0.82	–0.32
Syria	0.17	0.29	–0.13	0.00	0.54	**–0.54**
Taiwan	0.17	0.55	**–0.38**	0.67	0.86	–0.19
Thailand	0.83	0.55	0.28	0.67	0.87	–0.20
Austria	1.00	0.89	0.11	1.00	1.00	0.00
Belgium	1.00	0.93	0.07	1.00	(1.01)	–0.01
Cyprus	0.50	0.67	–0.17	1.00	0.93	0.07
Denmark	1.00	0.90	0.10	1.00	0.96	0.04
Finland	0.83	(1.04)	–0.20	1.00	(1.08)	–0.08
France	1.00	0.92	0.08	1.00	(1.01)	–0.01
West Germany	1.00	0.97	0.03	1.00	(1.05)	–0.05
Greece	0.83	0.65	0.18	1.00	0.71	0.29
Hungary	0.17	0.94	**–0.77**	1.00	0.83	0.17
Iceland	1.00	0.80	0.20	1.00	0.89	0.11
Ireland	1.00	0.90	0.10	1.00	1.00	0.00
Italy	1.00	0.88	0.12	1.00	0.96	0.04
Netherlands	1.00	0.92	0.08	1.00	0.97	0.03

Table 2.4 (continued)

Country	Democracy, 1975			Democracy, 1994		
	Actual	Projected	Gap	Actual	Projected	Gap
Norway	1.00	0.99	0.01	1.00	1.00	0.00
Poland	0.17	0.80	**−0.63**	0.83	0.86	−0.03
Portugal	0.33	0.73	**−0.40**	1.00	0.95	0.05
Spain	0.33	0.82	**−0.49**	1.00	0.99	0.01
Sweden	0.83	0.90	−0.07	1.00	0.98	0.02
Switzerland	1.00	(1.02)	−0.02	1.00	(1.06)	−0.06
Turkey	0.67	0.46	0.21	0.33	0.72	**−0.38**
United Kingdom	1.00	0.94	0.06	1.00	(1.02)	−0.02
Yugoslavia	0.17	0.65	**−0.48**	0.17	0.70	**−0.53**
Australia	1.00	0.92	0.08	1.00	1.00	0.00
Fiji	0.83	0.52	0.31	0.50	0.75	−0.25
New Zealand	1.00	0.89	0.11	1.00	0.95	0.05
Papua New Guinea	0.67	0.46	0.21	0.83	0.50	**0.33**

Note: Projected values are based on the estimated system shown in table 2.1, column 1. The 1975 projection is [1/(1 − coeff. of lagged democracy)] ∗ (estimated value based on other variables included in the 1975 equation). The 1994 projection is formed analogously. Values in parentheses are linearly fitted values that lie outside the range (0, 1). Values shown in boldface type have a magnitude of at least 0.33.

[a] Long-run projected value based on variables included in the 1980 equation.

between the current level of democracy and its long-run target. Values of the gap that exceed 0.33 in magnitude are shown in boldface type.

In 1975, out of 100 countries with data, 13 were below the long-run target for democracy by at least 0.33 and 5 were above by at least 0.33. In 1994, out of 102 places with data, 8 were below target by at least 0.33 and 12 were above target by at least 0.33. The larger relative number with positive gaps in 1994 than in 1975 reflects the global upward trend in democracy (figure 2.3), which has surpassed the trend in the model's target level of democracy.

One striking observation is that only two countries—China and Yugoslavia—appear with the same sign (negative) on both lists. With an estimated rate of convergence for democracy of about one-third per five-year period (from the coefficient on lagged democracy in column 1 of table 2.1), a lot of reversion to the mean occurs over nineteen years.

Among the African countries, Botswana, Gambia, and Mauritius looked "too democratic" in 1975, but the situation for Gambia changed with a coup in 1994. Botswana and Mauritius were still above target for democracy in 1994 but by smaller amounts than in 1975.

Several African countries, such as Benin and Rwanda, were surprisingly nondemocratic in 1975. However, a recent surge of democratization caused many of the African countries to become more democratic than predicted by 1994. This group includes Benin, Central African Republic, Guinea-Bissau, Malawi, Mali, Mozambique, Niger, and Zambia. In some of these cases, the democratization may be explicable from the pressures and rewards exerted by international organizations, such as the International Monetary Fund (IMF) and the World Bank. (The recent U.S. efforts in Haiti are analogous.)

In any case, the regression analysis predicts that, as with the African experience of the 1960s, democracy that gets well ahead of economic development will not last. (As a possible indicator of this process, Niger had a military coup in January 1996 and then became nondemocratic.) South Africa, which was below target for democracy in 1975, also became above target by 1994 and would be projected to become less democratic.

A few African countries still had below-target levels of democracy in 1994. Prominent here are Rwanda, Sudan, and Swaziland. (Nigeria and Somalia would likely be included in this category but have missing data and are therefore excluded from table 2.4.)

For Latin America in 1975, several countries were surprisingly nondemocratic, including Panama, Chile, Ecuador, and Uruguay. All of these places subsequently experienced sharp increases in political freedom. In 1994, Bolivia had far more democracy than would be predicted from its economic situation. Mexico was below target in 1994 and is predicted to become more democratic.

Among Asian countries, surprisingly low democracy prevailed in 1975 in Bangladesh, China, and Taiwan, but only China remained in this state in 1994. Hong Kong, Singapore, and Syria exhibited below-target democracy in 1994. The model predicts increases in democracy in these cases, but the model has not been informed of Hong Kong's post-1997 relationship with China. It will be of interest to see whether prosperous Singapore joins South Korea and Taiwan in their marked democratizations.

On the other side, democracy was higher than predicted for India and Indonesia in 1975. The Indian situation (along with that in Mauritius) accounted for the significance of the Hindu variable in the regression analysis. However, with the decline in Gastil's measure of democracy (in 1991 and 1993), India no longer looked like a large outlier in 1994. For Indonesia, the decline in democracy to zero in 1994 meant that it had fallen below target. Nepal had surprisingly high democracy in 1994.

Because of lack of data, only three countries from Central or Eastern Europe are represented in the sample: Hungary, Poland, and Yugoslavia. In each of these places, democracy was strikingly below its target level in 1975. Two countries in Western Europe—Portugal and Spain—were also surprisingly nondemocratic. By 1994, all of these countries except Yugoslavia had, as predicted, become far more democratic. Thus, these countries were no longer negative outliers in 1994; in fact, Hungary was more democratic than predicted. The model forecasts a large increase of democracy in Yugoslavia, which should perhaps now be identified with Serbia. The model also predicts substantial democratization for Turkey, which was surprisingly nondemocratic in 1994.

Some Conclusions

The positive relation between democracy and prior measures of prosperity—the Lipset hypothesis—is well established as an empirical regularity. Given the strength of this relation, it is surprising that convincing theoretical models of this mechanism do not exist. Thus, development of such a theory is a priority for future research. At the empirical level, it would be interesting to investigate the relation of democracy to inequality, colonial status, and religion. Of course, it may be that the development of satisfactory theories for the determination of democracy would also suggest additional empirical linkages that ought to be explored.

3   Inflation and Growth

In recent years, many central banks have placed increased emphasis on price stability. Monetary policy, whether expressed in terms of interest rates or growth of monetary aggregates, has been geared increasingly toward the achievement of low and stable inflation. Central bankers and most other observers view price stability as a worthy objective because they think that inflation is costly. Some of these costs involve the average rate of inflation, and others relate to the variability and uncertainty of inflation. But the general idea is that businesses and households are thought to perform poorly when inflation is high and unpredictable.

The academic literature contains a lot of theoretical work on the costs of inflation, as reviewed recently by Briault (1995). This analysis provides a presumption that inflation is a bad idea, but the case is not decisive without supporting empirical findings. Although some empirical results (also surveyed by Briault) suggest that inflation is harmful, the evidence is not overwhelming. It is therefore important to carry out additional empirical research on the relation between inflation and economic performance. This chapter explores this relation with the cross-country data used in the previous chapters.

Data on Inflation

Table 3.1 provides information about the behavior of inflation in the data set. Annual inflation rates were computed in most cases from consumer price indexes. (The deflator for the GDP was used for the few instances in which the data on consumer prices were unavailable.) The table shows the mean and median across the countries of the inflation rates in three decades: 1960–1970, 1970–1980, and 1980–1990. The median inflation rate was 3.3 percent per year in the 1960s (117 countries), 10.1 percent in the 1970s (122 countries), and 8.9 percent in the 1980s (119 countries). The upper panel of figure 3.1 provides a histogram for the inflation rates observed over the three decades. The bottom panel applies to the forty-four observations for which the inflation rate exceeded 20 percent per year.[1]

The annual data were used for each country over each decade to compute a measure of inflation variability, the standard deviation of the inflation rate around its decadal mean. Table 3.1 shows the mean and median of these standard deviations for the three decades. The median was 2.4 percent per year in the 1960s, 5.4 percent in the 1970s,

Table 3.1
Descriptive statistics on inflation

Variable	Mean	Median	Number of countries
1960–1970			
Inflation rate	.054	.033	117
Standard deviation of inflation rate	.039	.024	117
1970–1980			
Inflation rate	.133	.101	122
Standard deviation of inflation rate	.075	.054	122
1980–1990			
Inflation rate	.191	.089	119
Standard deviation of inflation rate	.134	.049	119

Notes: The inflation rate is computed on an annual basis for each country from data on consumer price indexes (from the World Bank, STARS databank and issues of *World Tables*; International Monetary Fund, *International Financial Statistics*, yearbook issues; and individual country sources). In a few cases, figures on the GDP deflator were used. The average inflation rate for each country in each decade is the mean of the annual rates. The standard deviation for each country in each decade is the square root of the average squared difference of the annual inflation rate from the decadal mean. The values shown for inflation in this table are the mean or median across the countries of the decade-average inflation rates. Similarly, the figures for standard deviations are the mean or median across the countries of the standard deviations for each decade.

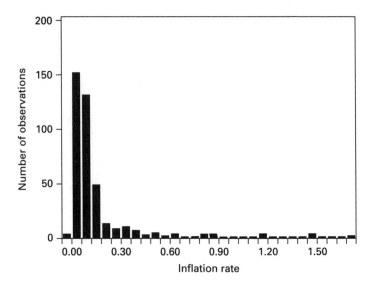

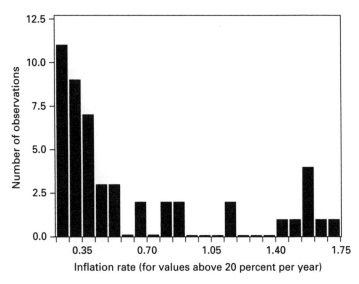

Figure 3.1
Histograms for inflation rate

and 4.9 percent in the 1980s. Thus, a rise in inflation variability accompanied the increase in the average inflation rate since the 1960s.

Figure 3.2 confirms the well-known view that a higher variability of inflation tends to accompany a higher average rate of inflation (see, for example, Okun 1971 and Logue and Willett 1976). These charts provide scatter plots of the standard deviation of inflation (measured for each country around its own decadal mean) against the average inflation rate (the mean of each country's inflation rate over the decade). The upper panel considers only inflation rates below 15 percent per year, the middle panel includes values above 15 percent per year, and the lower panel covers the entire range. The positive, but imperfect, relation between variability and mean is apparent throughout.

Preliminary Results for the Effect of Inflation on Economic Growth

To get a first-pass estimate of the effect of inflation on economic growth, the inflation rate was included over each period as an explanatory variable along with the other growth determinants considered in chapter 1. The system shown in column 1 of table 3.2 is the same as that from column 1 of table 1.1, except for the instruments associated with inflation. The estimation reported in column 1 of table 3.2 includes contemporaneous inflation among the instruments, whereas that in table 1.1 uses alternative instruments, as described later. The estimated coefficient of

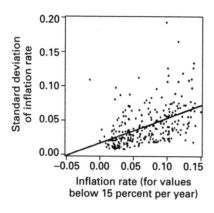

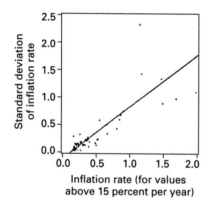

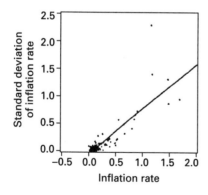

Figure 3.2
Standard deviation of inflation versus mean inflation

inflation in table 3.2, column 1 is significantly negative: −0.029 (0.004).[2] Hence, an increase by 10 percentage points in the annual inflation rate is associated on impact with a decline by 0.3 percentage point in the annual growth rate of GDP.

Figure 3.3 depicts graphically the relation between growth and inflation. The horizontal axis plots the inflation rate; each observation corresponds to the average rate for a particular country over one of the time periods considered (1965–1975, 1975–1985, and 1985–1990). The top panel in the chart considers inflation rates below 20 percent per year, the middle panel contains values above 20 percent per year, and the bottom panel covers the full range of inflation. As usual, the vertical axis plots the growth rate of GDP, net of the part of the growth rate that is explained by all of the explanatory variables aside from the inflation rate.[3] Thus, the panels illustrate the relation between growth and inflation after all of the other growth determinants have been held constant.

The panels of figure 3.3 show regression lines (least-squares lines) through the scatter plots. The slope of the line in the lowest panel corresponds approximately to the significantly negative coefficient shown in column 1 of table 3.2. The panels show, however, that the fit is dominated by the inverse relation between growth and inflation at high rates of inflation. For inflation rates below 20 percent per year, as shown in the top panel, the relation between growth and inflation is not statistically significant.

Table 3.2
Alternative specifications for inflation in growth regressions

Independent variable	(1)	(2)	(3)	(4)
Log(GDP)	−.0260	−.0261	−.0261	−.0262
	(.0031)	(.0031)	(.0031)	(.0031)
Male schooling	.0116	.0114	.0111	.0110
	(.0024)	(.0024)	(.0025)	(.0025)
Log(life expectancy)	.0421	.0419	.0418	.0427
	(.0137)	(.0137)	(.0139)	(.0139)
Log(GDP) * male schooling	−.0057	−.0057	−.0052	−.0052
	(.0016)	(.0016)	(.0017)	(.0017)
Log(fertility rate)	−.0166	−.0167	−.0170	−.0167
	(.0053)	(.0053)	(.0054)	(.0054)
Government consumption ratio	−.138	−.140	−.137	−.140
	(.026)	(.026)	(.026)	(.026)
Rule of law index	.0310	.0310	.0315	.0317
	(.0053)	(.0053)	(.0054)	(.0054)
Terms of trade change	.137	.137	.139	.139
	(.030)	(.030)	(.030)	(.030)
Democracy index	.091	.091	.104	.103
	(.026)	(.026)	(.026)	(.026)
Democracy index squared	−.088	−.088	−.099	−.097
	(.023)	(.023)	(.023)	(.023)
Inflation rate	−.0293	−.0317	−.0261	−.0314
	(.0043)	(.0080)	(.0054)	(.0113)
Standard deviation of inflation rate		.0030		.0071
		(.0089)		(.0150)
R^2	.56, .51, .50	.56, .51, .50	.55, .49, .51	.55, .50, .50
No. of observations	80, 87, 84	80, 87, 84	80, 87, 84	80, 87, 84

Notes: The systems correspond to those shown in table 1.1 except for the inflation variables. In columns 1 and 2, the actual inflation rate over each period is included on the instrument list. Columns 3 and 4 include lagged inflation (for 1960–1965, 1970–1975, and 1980–1985, respectively) and its square, but not contemporaneous inflation, with the instruments. Columns 2 and 4 add the standard deviation of the inflation rate for 1965–1975, 1975–1985, and 1985–1990, respectively. Column 2 includes this standard deviation on the instrument list. Column 4 includes only the lagged standard deviation (for 1960–1965, 1970–1975, and 1980–1985) with the instruments.

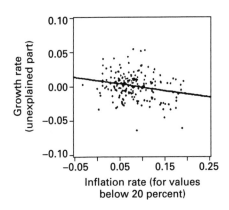

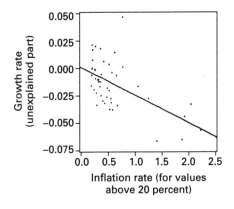

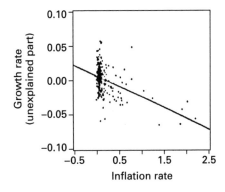

Figure 3.3
Growth rate versus inflation rate

The results indicate that there is not enough information in the low-inflation experiences to isolate precisely the effect of inflation on growth, but they do not necessarily mean that this effect is small at low rates of inflation. To check for linearity of the relation between growth and inflation, the system was reestimated for the whole sample with separate coefficients for inflation in three ranges: up to 15 percent, between 15 and 40 percent, and over 40 percent. The estimated coefficients on inflation in this form are −0.023 (0.036) in the low range, −0.055 (0.017) in the middle range, and −0.029 (0.005) in the upper range. Thus, the clear evidence for the negative relation between growth and inflation comes from the middle and upper intervals. However, since the three estimated coefficients do not differ significantly from each other (p value $= 0.12$), the data are consistent with a linear relationship. In particular, the data would not reject the hypothesis that the relation between growth and inflation is negative at low rates of inflation and of the same magnitude as that for higher rates of inflation. Moreover, there is no sign in any range of a positive relation, which would signify that higher inflation had to be tolerated to obtain more growth.

Although statistically significant effects arise only when the high-inflation experiences are included, the results are not sensitive to a few outlier observations. Table 3.3 shows the twenty-seven cases of inflation in excess of 40 percent per year for one of the time periods: 1965–1975, 1975–1985, and 1985–1990. Note that Uruguay appears three times (although it is by no means the overall champion for high

Table 3.3
High-inflation observations

Country	Inflation rate
1965–1975	
Chile	0.68
Indonesia	0.53
Uruguay	0.50
1975–1985	
Argentina	1.26
Bolivia	1.06
Brazil	0.66
Haiti	0.48
Israel	0.78
Peru	0.56
Uganda	0.53
Uruguay	0.41
Zaire	0.44
1985–1990	
Argentina	1.92
Brazil	2.04
Guinea-Bissau [a]	0.53
Mexico	0.53
Mozambique [a]	0.48
Nicaragua	1.87
Peru	2.22
Poland [a]	0.81
Sierra Leone	0.63
Turkey	0.43
Uganda	0.78
Uruguay	0.58
Yugoslavia	1.41
Zaire	0.59
Zambia	0.56

Note: Period-average inflation rate exceeds 40 percent per year.

[a] Not included in the regression sample because of missing data on other variables.

inflation), and Argentina, Brazil, Peru, Uganda, and Zaire show up twice each. The other countries, with one observation each, are Chile, Indonesia, Bolivia, Haiti, Israel, Guinea-Bissau, Mexico, Mozambique, Nicaragua, Poland, Sierra Leone, Turkey, Yugoslavia, and Zambia. (Guinea-Bissau, Mozambique, and Poland are not in the regression sample because of missing data on other variables.) The exclusion of any small number of these high-inflation observations—Nicaragua and Zaire were suggested by Bruno and Easterly (1995)—has a negligible effect on the results.

The estimates are also reasonably stable over time. If different coefficients for inflation are allowed for each period but the system is otherwise the same as in column 1 of table 3.2, then the resulting estimates are -0.040 (0.015) for 1965–1975, -0.040 (0.010) for 1975–1985, and -0.026 (0.005) for 1985–1990. These values do not differ significantly from each other (p value $= 0.29$).

The standard deviation of inflation can be added to the system to see whether inflation variability has a relation with growth when the average inflation rate is held constant. The strong positive correlation between the mean and variability of inflation (figure 3.2) suggests that it would be difficult to distinguish the influences of these two aspects of inflation. However, when the two variables are entered jointly into the regression system in column 2 of table 3.2, the estimated coefficient on inflation remains similar to that found before (-0.032 [0.008]), and the estimated coefficient on the standard deviation of inflation is essentially zero (0.003 [0.009]).[4]

Thus, for a given average rate of inflation, the variability of inflation has no significant relation with growth. One possible interpretation of this result is that the realized variability of inflation does not adequately measure the uncertainty of inflation, the variable that one would have expected to be negatively related to growth. This issue is worth further investigation.

The Endogeneity of Inflation

The key problem in interpreting the effect of inflation on growth from column 1 of table 3.2 is that the regression need not reflect causation from inflation to growth. Inflation is an endogenous variable, which may respond to growth or to other variables related to growth. For example, an inverse relation between growth and inflation would arise if an exogenous slowing of the growth rate tended to generate higher inflation. This increase in inflation could result if monetary authorities reacted to economic slowdowns with expansionary policies. Moreover, if the path of monetary aggregates did not change, then the equality between money supply and demand at each point in time implies that a reduction in the growth rate of output would tend automatically to raise the inflation rate.

Kocherlakota (1996) focused on this last source of endogeneity bias. To fix ideas, suppose as he does that the money growth rate, μ_t, is determined exogenously. The relation between the inflation rate, π_t, and μ_t is given from the money-supply-equals-money-demand condition by

$$\pi_t = \mu_t - g_t + v_t, \tag{3.1}$$

where g_t is the growth rate of output and v_t is an independent shock to velocity. Suppose that the effect of inflation on the growth rate is described by

$$g_t = -\alpha \pi_t + \epsilon_t, \tag{3.2}$$

where ϵ_t is an independent shock and α is the coefficient to be estimated.

In this framework, the OLS regression coefficient, $\hat{\alpha}$, of g_t on π_t can be shown to be given by

$$\hat{\alpha} = -\left\{ \frac{\alpha \cdot [VAR(\mu) + VAR(v)] + VAR(\epsilon)}{VAR(\mu) + VAR(v) + VAR(\epsilon)} \right\}. \tag{3.3}$$

Thus, $\hat{\alpha}$ will be close to α if the variances of the shocks to money growth and velocity are much greater than those to output growth.

Using averages over the three periods in the panel and measuring money by either M1 or M2, I find that $VAR(\mu) \approx .032$, $VAR(v) \approx .004$, and $VAR(\epsilon) \approx .0002$. Then a value $\alpha = 0$ corresponds to $\hat{\alpha} \approx -.006$, and a value $\alpha = -.020$ to $\hat{\alpha} \approx -.026$. Hence, the likely bias would be small and could not account for the empirical findings on inflation in column 1 of table 3.2. Moreover, if inflation, rather than money growth, were determined exogenously, then the bias would be nil.

The Kocherlakota argument also implies that the results would be very different if money growth, rather than inflation, were included in the growth regressions. If the panel estimation from column 1 of table 3.2 is redone with M1 growth replacing the inflation rate, then the estimated coefficient is −0.0306 (0.0055). If M2 growth is used instead, the result is −0.0280 (0.0055). Thus, this direct procedure verifies that the magnitude of the estimated coefficient is similar when money growth, rather than inflation, is used as the regressor. Basically the results reveal an inverse relation between the growth rate of GDP and the growth rate of prices *or* money. The distinction between inflation and money growth is not central to the findings.

Another possibility is that some omitted third variable is correlated with growth and inflation. For example, better enforcement of property rights is likely to spur investment and growth and is also likely to accompany a rules-based setup in which the monetary authority generates a lower average rate of inflation. The idea is that a committed monetary policy represents the application of the rule of law to the behavior of the monetary authority. Some of the explanatory variables in the system attempt to capture the degree of maintenance of the rule of law. However, to the extent that these measures are imperfect, the inflation rate may proxy inversely for the rule of law and thereby show up as a negative influence on growth. The estimated coefficient on the inflation rate could therefore reflect an effect on growth that has nothing to do with inflation per se.

Some researchers like to handle this type of problem by using some variant of fixed-effects estimation, that is, by allowing for an individual constant for each country. This procedure basically eliminates cross-sectional information about inflation from the sample and therefore relies on effects within countries from changes over time of inflation and other variables. It is not apparent that problems of correlation of inflation with omitted variables would be less serious in this time-series context than in cross sections. (If a country is undergoing an inflation crisis or implementing a monetary reform, then it is likely to be experiencing other crises or reforms at the same time.) Moreover, the problems with measurement error and timing of relationships would be more substantial in the time series. The one thing that is clear is that fixed-effects procedures lose a lot of information.

Another way to proceed is to find satisfactory instrumental variables: reasonably exogenous variables that are themselves significantly related to inflation. My search along these lines proceeded along the sequence now described.

Central Bank Independence

One promising source of instruments for inflation involves legal provisions that guarantee more or less central bank independence. A recent literature (Bade and Parkin 1982; Grilli, Masciandaro, and Tabellini 1991; Cukierman 1992; Alesina and Summers 1993) argues that a greater degree of independence leads to lower average rates of money growth and inflation and to greater monetary stability. The idea is that independence enhances the ability of the central bank to commit to price stability and, hence, to deliver low and stable inflation. (This view assumes that central bankers have relatively strong preferences for low inflation.) Alesina and Summers (1993, figs. 1a, 1b) find striking negative relationships among sixteen developed countries from 1955 to 1988 between an index of the degree of central bank independence and the mean and variance of inflation. Thus, in their context, the measure of central bank independence satisfies one condition needed for a good inflation instrument; it has substantial explanatory power for inflation.

Because of the difficulty of enacting changes in laws, it is plausible that a good deal of the cross-country differences in legal provisions that influence central bank independence can be treated as exogenous. Problems arise, however, if the legal framework changes in response to inflation (although the sign of this interaction is unclear). In addition, exogeneity would be violated if alterations in a country's legal environment for monetary policy are correlated with changes in unmeasured institutional features, such as structures that maintain property rights, that influence growth rates. This problem is, however, mitigated by the inclusion of other explanatory variables, notably the index of the rule of law, in the regression framework.

Cukierman (1992, chap. 19) argues that the legal provisions that govern central bank action differ substantially from the way that the banks actually operate. In particular, he distinguishes the legal term of office of the central bank governor from the observed turnover. The latter variable would be more closely related to bank performance (and hence to inflation), but cannot be treated as exogenous to growth or omitted third variables. Thus, for the purpose of constructing instruments for inflation, the preferred strategy is to focus on the extent to which inflation can be explained by differences in legal provisions for the central bank.

Table 3.4 shows an index of central bank independence for sixty-seven countries, based on the information compiled by Cukierman (1992, chap. 19, appendix A) over time periods that correspond roughly to the four decades from the 1950s to the 1980s. The index is an average over the time periods and for numerous categories of legal provisions contained in the charters of the central banks (see the notes to the table). The details of construction differ somewhat from those used by Cukierman, but the values shown in the table are similar to those reported in his table 19.3 for the 1980s.

Table 3.4 also contains the average inflation rate from 1960 to 1990 for the sixty-seven countries in my sample that have data on the index of central bank independence. A comparison between the index and the inflation rate reveals a crucial problem: the correlation between the two variables is essentially zero, as is clear from figure 3.4. This verdict is also maintained if one looks separately over the three decades from the 1960s to the 1980s and if one holds constant other possible determinants of inflation. In this broad sample of countries, differences in legal provisions that ought to affect

Table 3.4
Inflation rates and central bank independence

Country	Index of bank independence	Inflation rate 1960–1990
West Germany	0.71	0.037
Switzerland	0.65	0.038
Austria	0.65	0.043
Egypt	0.57	0.094
Denmark	0.53	0.069
Costa Rica	0.52	0.117
Greece	0.52	0.109
United States	0.51	0.049
Ethiopia	0.50	0.058
Ireland	0.50	0.083
Philippines	0.49	0.107
Bahamas	0.48	0.063 [a]
Tanzania	0.48	0.133
Nicaragua	0.47	0.436
Israel	0.47	0.350
Netherlands	0.47	0.045
Canada	0.47	0.054
Venezuela	0.45	0.100
Barbados	0.44	0.075
Argentina	0.44	0.891
Honduras	0.44	0.058
Peru	0.44	0.606
Chile	0.43	0.416
Turkey	0.42	0.235
Malta	0.42	0.035
Iceland	0.42	0.229
Kenya	0.40	0.082
Luxembourg	0.40	0.044
Zaire	0.39	0.357
Mexico	0.37	0.227

Table 3.4 (continued)

Country	Index of bank independence	Inflation rate 1960–1990
Indonesia	0.36	0.366
Botswana	0.36	0.076
Ghana	0.35	0.256
France	0.34	0.064
Zambia	0.34	0.174
South Africa	0.33	0.099
Nigeria	0.33	0.125
Malaysia	0.32	0.034
Uganda	0.32	0.353
Italy	0.31	0.088
Finland	0.30	0.073
Sweden	0.30	0.067
Singapore	0.30	0.034
India	0.30	0.074
United Kingdom	0.30	0.077
South Korea	0.29	0.113
China	0.29	0.039
Bolivia	0.29	0.466
Uruguay	0.29	0.441
Brazil	0.28	0.723
Australia	0.27	0.067
Thailand	0.27	0.052
Western Samoa	0.26	0.112 [b]
New Zealand	0.25	0.085
Nepal	0.23	0.084
Panama	0.23	0.033
Zimbabwe	0.22	0.074
Hungary	0.21	0.047
Japan	0.20	0.054
Pakistan	0.19	0.072

Table 3.4 (continued)

Country	Index of bank independence	Inflation rate 1960–1990
Colombia	0.19	0.170
Spain	0.16	0.096
Morocco	0.15	0.055
Belgium	0.13	0.048
Yugoslavia	0.12	0.395
Poland	0.12	0.293 [a]
Norway	0.12	0.066

Notes: The index of central bank independence is computed from data in Cukierman (1992, chapter 19, appendix A). The index is a weighted average of the available data from 1950 to 1989 of legal provisions regarding (1) appointment and dismissal of the governor (weight 1/6), (2) procedures for the formulation of monetary policy (weight 1/6), (3) objectives of central bank policy (weight 1/6), and (4) limitations on lending by the central bank (weight 1/2). The first category is an unweighted average of three underlying variables that involve the governor's term of office and the procedures for appointment and dismissal. The second category is an unweighted average of two variables—one indicating the location of the authority for setting monetary policy and the other specifying methods for resolving conflicts about policy. The third category relates to the prominence attached to price stability in the bank's charter. The fourth category is an unweighted average of four variables: limitations on advances, limitations on securitized lending, an indicator for the location of the authority that prescribes lending terms, and the circle of potential borrowers from the central bank. For each underlying variable, Cukierman defines a scale from 0 to 1, where 0 indicates least favorable to central bank independence and 1 indicates most favorable. The overall index shown in the table runs correspondingly from 0 to 1. See table 2.4 for a discussion of the inflation data.

[a] 1970–1990.
[b] 1975–1990.

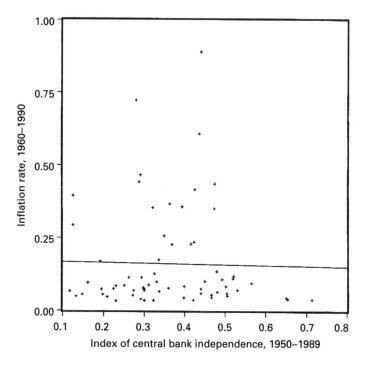

Figure 3.4
Inflation and central bank independence

central bank independence have no explanatory power for inflation.[5]

The Alesina-Summers (1993) finding of a close negative link between inflation and central bank independence turns out to be a fragile one. In their sample of sixteen developed countries, the correlation between average inflation (between 1960 and 1990) and their measure of independence

is −0.82. If one retains their sample but switches to the pre-
sumably more accurate indicator of independence based on
Cukierman's (1992) information, then the correlation falls
in magnitude to −0.59. If one sticks to developed countries
but enlarges the sample to the twenty-three OECD countries for which Cukierman had data on independence, then
the size of the correlation declines further to −0.18. (Ice-
land is particularly troublesome in this sample.) Finally, if
one considers the full sample of sixty-seven countries with
data (as in figure 3.4), then the correlation becomes a negligible −0.02.

This negative finding about the role of central bank independence is of considerable interest because it suggests that
low inflation cannot be attained merely by instituting legal
changes that appear to promote a more independent central bank. However, the result also means that we have to
search further for instruments to clarify the relation between
growth and inflation.[6]

Lagged Inflation

Earlier values of a country's inflation rate have substantial
explanatory power for inflation.[7] Lagged inflation would
also be exogenous with respect to innovations in subsequent
growth rates. Hence, if lagged inflation is used as an instrument, then the estimated relation between growth and inflation would not tend to reflect the short-run reverse effect of
growth on inflation.

One problem, however, is that lagged inflation would reflect persistent characteristics of a country's monetary institutions (such as the extent to which policymakers have credibility), and these characteristics could be correlated with omitted variables that are relevant to growth (such as the extent to which political institutions support the maintenance of property rights). The use of lagged inflation as an instrument would therefore not rule out the problems of interpretation that derive from omitted third variables. However, the inclusion of the other explanatory variables in the regression framework lessens this problem. Another favorable element is that the residuals from the growth equations are not significantly correlated over the time periods.

Column 3 of table 3.2 shows the estimated effect of inflation on the growth rate when lagged inflation (over the five years prior to each sample period) and its square are used as instruments. The estimated coefficient is -0.026 (0.005), slightly smaller in magnitude than that found in column 1 when contemporaneous inflation is included as an instrument. Thus, it seems that most of the estimated negative relation between growth and inflation does not represent reverse short-term (negative) effects of growth on inflation.

The significant negative influence of inflation on growth still shows up only when the high-inflation observations are included. The results are, however, again consistent with a linear relation and with stability over the time periods. The standard deviation of inflation also remains insignificant if it is added to the regressions (column 4 of table 3.2).

Prior Colonial Status

Another possible instrument for inflation comes from the observation that prior colonial status has substantial explanatory power for inflation. Table 3.5 breaks down averages of inflation rates from 1960 to 1990 by groups of countries classified, as in chapter 2, as noncolonies and former colonies of Britain, France, Spain or Portugal, and other countries (in this sample, Australia, Belgium, the Netherlands, New Zealand, and the United States).

Table 3.5 indicates that the average inflation rate for all 117 countries from 1960 to 1990 was 12.6 percent per year. The average for the 30 noncolonies of 8.9 percent was similar to that of 10.4 percent for the 42 British colonies and 6.6 percent for the 20 French colonies. However, the rates were strikingly higher for the 18 Spanish or Portuguese colonies—29.4 percent—and somewhat higher for the 7 other colonies—16.1 percent.

A key reason for the low average inflation rate in the former French colonies is the participation of most of the sub-Saharan African states in the fixed-exchange rate regime of the CFA franc (le franc des Colonies Françaises d'Afrique).[8] This type of reasonably exogenous commitment to relatively low inflation is exactly the kind of experiment that provides for a good instrument for inflation.

For many of the former British colonies, a significant element may be their prior experience with British organized

Table 3.5
Inflation rates and prior colonial status

Period	All countries	Noncolony	British colony	French colony	Spanish or Portuguese colony	Other colony	addendum: Latin Amer. not Spanish or Portuguese colony
1960–1970	.054 (121)	.045 (31)	.033 (43)	.030 (21)	.089 (19)	.194 (7)	.031 (7)
1970–1980	.131 (131)	.110 (32)	.120 (50)	.093 (20)	.218 (21)	.147 (8)	.109 (11)
1980–1990	.182 (132)	.124 (31)	.139 (51)	.074 (22)	.523 (20)	.136 (8)	.097 (11)
1960–1990	.126 (117)	.089 (30)	.104 (42)	.066 (20)	.294 (18)	.161 (7)	.090 (7)

Notes: The numbers shown in parentheses are the numbers of countries with available data that fall into each category. See table 3.1 for a discussion of the inflation data. Countries that were independent before 1776 are treated as noncolonies. Otherwise the colonial status refers to the most recent outside power; for example, the Philippines is attributed to the United States rather than Spain; Rwanda and Burundi are attributed to Belgium rather than Germany; and the Dominican Republic is attributed to France rather than Spain. Some countries that were dominated by other countries for some periods are treated as noncolonies; examples are Hungary, Poland, South Korea, and Taiwan. The only current colony in the sample is Hong Kong. The last column refers to countries that are located in Latin America but are not former Spanish or Portuguese colonies.

currency boards, another system that tends to generate low inflation (see Schwartz 1993). These boards involved, at one time or another before independence, most of the British colonies in Africa, the Caribbean, Southeast Asia, and the Middle East.

The high average inflation rate for the 16 former Spanish colonies in the sample does not reflect, per se, their presence in Latin America. For seven Latin American countries that are not former Spanish or Portuguese colonies,[9] the average inflation rate for 1960–1990 was only 9.0 percent, virtually the same as that for the noncolonies (see table 3.5). Also, four former Portuguese colonies in Africa experienced the relatively high average inflation rate of around 20 percent.[10] For Portugal and Spain themselves, the average inflation rate of 10.9 percent for 1960–1990 was well below the rate of 29.4 percent experienced by their former colonies. However, 10.9 percent inflation was higher than that experienced by France (6.4 percent) and the United Kingdom (7.7 percent).

The regression system focused on in chapter 1, shown in column 1 of table 1.1, shows the estimated effect of inflation on the growth rate of GDP when the instruments exclude contemporaneous or lagged inflation but include indicators of prior colonial status. The two variables used are a dummy for whether the country is a former Spanish or Portuguese colony and a dummy for whether the country is a former colony of a country other than Britain, France, Spain, or Portugal.[11] The estimated coefficient on the inflation rate is now −0.043 (0.008), higher in magnitude than that found in table 3.2 when contemporaneous or lagged inflation is used as an instrument. The significantly negative relation between growth and inflation again arises only when the high-inflation experiences are included in the sample. The results also continue to be stable over the time periods.

One question about the procedure is whether prior colonial status works in the growth regressions only because it serves as an imperfect proxy for Latin America, a region that is known to have experienced surprisingly weak economic growth (see, for example, the results in Barro 1991). However, column 2 of table 1.1 showed that if a dummy variable for Latin America is included in the system (along with dummies for sub-Saharan Africa and East Asia), then the estimated coefficient of inflation changes little: −0.039 (0.008). Moreover, the estimated coefficient on the Latin America dummy is not statistically significant at conventional levels: −0.0054 (0.0032). The results are basically the same if the Latin America dummy is added to the system from column 1 of table 3.2, in which contemporaneous inflation is used as an instrument. It therefore appears that much of the estimated effect of a Latin America dummy on growth rates in previous research reflected a proxying of this dummy for high inflation. In particular, the negative effect of inflation on growth does not just reflect the tendency of many high-inflation countries to be in Latin America.

Summary Findings on Inflation

A major result is that the estimated effect of inflation on growth is significantly negative when some plausible instruments are used in the statistical procedures. Thus, there is some reason to believe that the relations reflect causation from higher long-term inflation to reduced growth.

It should be stressed that the clear evidence for adverse effects of inflation comes from the experiences of high inflation. The magnitudes of effects are also not that large; for example, an increase in the average inflation rate by 10 percentage points per year is estimated to lower the growth rate of real per capita GDP on impact by 0.3 to 0.4 percentage point per year.

Some people have reacted to these kinds of findings by expressing skepticism about the value of cross-country empirical work. In fact, the wide differences in inflation experiences offered by this kind of panel provide the best opportunity for ascertaining the long-term effects of inflation and other variables on economic performance. If the effects cannot be detected accurately with these data, then they probably cannot be pinpointed anywhere else. In particular, the usual focus on annual or quarterly time series of thirty to forty years for one or a few countries is much less promising.

In any event, the apparently small estimated effects of inflation on growth are misleading. Over long periods, these changes in growth rates have dramatic effects on standards of living. For example, a reduction in the growth rate by 0.3 to 0.4 percentage point per year (produced on impact by 10 percentage points more of average inflation) means that the level of real GDP would be lowered after thirty years by 6 to 9 percent.[12] In 1996, the U.S. gross domestic product was around $8 trillion; 6 to 9 percent of this amount is $480 to $720 billion, more than enough to justify a keen interest in price stability.

Concluding
Observations

The data now available for a broad panel of countries over thirty years provide the information necessary to isolate determinants of economic growth. With respect to government policies, the evidence indicates that the growth rate of real per capita GDP is enhanced by better maintenance of the rule of law, smaller government consumption, and lower inflation. Increases in political rights initially increase growth but tend to retard growth once a moderate level of democracy has been attained. Growth is also stimulated by greater starting levels of life expectancy and of male secondary and higher schooling, lower fertility rates, and improvements in the terms of trade. For given values of these variables, growth is higher if a country begins with a lower starting level of real per capita GDP; that is, the data reveal a pattern of conditional convergence.

To some extent, the forces that have been isolated in this and other empirical studies reflect the variables that researchers have been able to measure in a consistent and reasonably accurate manner for a large number of countries. Additional public policies that are likely to be important for growth include tax distortions; public pension and other transfer programs; and regulations that affect labor, financial, and other markets. Also likely to be important are infrastructure investments, R&D outlays, the quality of education, and the distribution of income and wealth. Some of these elements have been discussed in other empirical studies, but further measurement and investigation is important for obtaining reliable results.

The great strength of the cross-country approach is that it provides the breadth of experience needed to assess government policies and other determinants of long-term economic growth. At the same time, the use of these data creates problems related to measurement and estimation. Many critics of cross-country empirical work focus on these difficulties, but my view is that the informational benefits override these objections. Naturally this viewpoint will become more persuasive if further progress can be made in overcoming the problems of measurement and estimation.

Notes

Chapter 1

1. With exogenous, labor-augmenting technological progress, the level of output per worker grows in the long run, but the level of output per effective worker approaches a constant, y^*. Hence, y^* should be interpreted in this generalized sense.

2. The data on real per capita GDP are the internationally comparable values generated by Summers and Heston (1993). The vertical axis in figure 1.1 contains observations on per capita growth rates for 1965–1975, 1975–1985, and 1985–1990, the three periods used in the detailed empirical analysis described in this chapter. The horizontal axis shows the corresponding values of the logarithm of per capita GDP in 1965, 1975, and 1985.

3. The data and detailed definitions of the variables are contained in the Barro-Lee data set, which is available on the Internet from the National Bureau of Economic Research (nber.harvard.edu) and the World Bank (www.worldbank.org/html/prdmg/grthweb/ddbarle2.htm).

4. Most of the GDP figures are from version 5.6 of the Summers-Heston data set (see Summers and Heston 1991, 1993 for general descriptions). World Bank figures on real GDP growth rates (based on domestic accounts only) are used for 1985–1990 when the Summers-Heston figures are unavailable.

5. The variable log(GDP) in table 1.1 refers to 1965 in the first period, 1975 in the second period, and 1985 in the third period. Five-year earlier values of log(GDP) are used as instruments. The use of these instruments lessens the estimation problems associated with temporary measurement error in GDP.

6. A full treatment of convergence would also require an analysis of how the various explanatory variables—such as schooling, health, and fertility—respond to the development of the economy.

7. This result is only approximate because the growth rate is observed as an average over ten or five years rather than at a point in time. The implied instantaneous rate of convergence is slightly higher than the value indicated by the coefficient. See Barro and Sala-i-Martin (1995, chap. 2) for a discussion.

8. The residual is calculated from the regression system that contains all of the variables, including the log of initial GDP. But the contribution from initial GDP is left out to compute the variable on the vertical axis in the scatter diagram. The residual has also been normalized to have a zero mean. The fitted straight line shown in the figure comes from an ordinary-least-squares (OLS) regression of the residual on the log of initial GDP. Therefore, the slope of the line differs somewhat from the regression coefficient shown in table 1.1.

9. The results are similar if the infant mortality rate is used instead of life expectancy as a measure of health status.

10. Schooling of those aged twenty-five and over has somewhat more explanatory power than schooling of those aged fifteen and over.

11. In earlier results, Barro and Lee (1994) found that the estimated coefficient on female secondary and higher schooling was significantly negative. With the revised data on education, the estimated female coefficents are essentially zero.

12. The constant term is the one applicable to the 1985–1990 equation. More accurate growth forecasts might be obtainable from a full vector-autoregressive (VAR) system that relates all variables to lagged observations.

13. Jordan could be included as the eighty-seventh country and actually has the highest growth forecast: 6.9 percent per year. However, Jordan was omitted from table 1.4 because the data for the West Bank are intermingled with those for Jordan proper.

Chapter 2

1. Putnam's (1993) empirical work is, however, marred by his tendency to identify good government with big government.

2. See Gastil (1991) for a discussion of the methods that underlie his data series. Inkeles (1991) provides an overview of measurement issues on democracy. He finds (p. x) a "high degree of agreement produced by the classification of nations as democratic or not, even when democracy is measured in somewhat different ways by different analysts." Bollen (1990) suggests that his measures are reasonably comparable to Gastil's. It is difficult to check comparability directly because the two series do not overlap in time. Moreover, many countries, especially those in Africa, clearly experienced major declines in the extent of democracy from the 1960s to the 1970s. Thus, no direct inference about comparability can be made from the higher average of Bollen's figures for the 1960s than for Gastil's numbers for the 1970s.

3. See Sirowy and Inkeles (1990) and Przeworski and Limongi (1993) for broad surveys of this kind of empirical evidence.

4. The conclusions are similar if dummy variables for different intervals of the democracy indicator are employed. (Note that the underlying indicator may have only an ordinal meaning.) For example, if the indicator is divided into three regions—up to 0.33,

between 0.33 and 0.67, and greater than 0.67—then the estimated effect on growth is highest in the middle range and roughly similar in the two extreme ranges.

5. The residual is calculated from the regression system that contains all of the variables, including democracy and its square. But the contributions from the two democracy variables are left out to compute the variable on the vertical axis. This residual has also been normalized to have a zero mean. The curve shown in the figure comes from an OLS regression of the residual on democracy and its square.

6. The empirical results turn out to be virtually the same if contemporaneous values of the Z variables are entered into equation 2.1 (that is, if the lag T is set to zero), but lagged values of democracy and the Z variables are used as instruments.

7. The democracy indicator takes on only seven discrete values between 0 and 1, but the linear specification on the right-hand side does not take this pattern into account. In practice, none of the fitted values turned out to be negative, and only a few exceeded 1.0. The highest fitted value, 1.04, applies to the United States in 1994.

8. The results are basically the same if the infant mortality rate is used instead of life expectancy.

9. The IMF definition includes countries whose net oil exports represent a minimum of two-thirds of total exports and are at least equivalent to approximately 1 percent of world exports of oil. A definition based on membership in the Organization of Petroleum Exporting Countries would add Ecuador and omit Bahrain and Oman.

10. The standard figures on urbanization, which are reported by the World Bank and used here, suffer from inconsistent definitions of urbanization across countries.

11. Primary schooling of males and females aged fifteen and over has slightly more explanatory power than primary schooling of those aged twenty-five and over.

12. Similarly, Helliwell (1994, table 1) finds that the Gastil measures of political rights and civil liberties are positively related to levels of GDP and secondary school enrollment ratios.

13. Data were provided by the World Bank and originate from Jain (1975) and Lecaillon et al. (1984). For a discussion of the data, see Perotti (1996).

14. The value 1 can be thought of as the effective years of educational human capital possessed by a person with no formal schooling.

15. The underlying data, from the *World Christian Encyclopedia* (Barrett 1982), are estimates of professed affiliation in 1970 and 1980. (Figures are also available for 1900.) This information takes no account of regularity of church attendance or amounts spent on religious activities. The data provided in the encyclopedia are compiled from the most authoritative local sources, published or unpublished, including government censuses of religion. A large part of the data was collected directly by the editors, who visited virtually all of the countries over the years 1965–1975. The basic concept of a religious adherent is that the person professes to believe in the religion when government censuses or public opinion polls ask the question, "What is your religion?" Each person is considered to have at most one religious affiliation. Further work on cross-country religion data is ongoing.

16. The system allows for some variation over time in religious affiliation in that the 1970 religion figures appear in the first three equations for democracy, and the 1980 figures enter into the last three equations. In most cases, however, the variations in religious affiliation between 1970 and 1980 are minor. If the 1970 values are

included in all six eqations, then the results are virtually indistinguishable from those shown in regression 9 of table 2.2.

17. The 1980 value of nonreligion for China is 0.71. The other values that exceed 0.1 are 0.35 for Uruguay; 0.29 for Sweden; 0.17 for
Yugoslavia; 0.16 for Italy, Hungary, and France; 0.15 for Australia;
0.14 for Hong Kong; and 0.12 for the Netherlands and Japan.

18. A formal test rejects equality of the coefficients in the systems
for democracy and civil liberties. Viewed individually, the only
coefficients that are found to differ significantly are those for life
expectancy, male schooling, population, and the constant term.

19. More precisely, the model shows how initial democracy and the
values of the other explanatory variables influence the probabili-
ties of transition over time among the seven discrete rankings of
democracy.

20. A positive trend in GDP and the other indicators of prosperity
implies an upward trend in democracy. This result seems reasonable because—when evaluated in terms of the Gastil concept of
political participation—there have not been many full democracies
in the world until the twentieth century.

21. The projected value equals [1/(1 − coefficient of lagged democracy)]∗(estimated value based on explanatory variables other than
lagged democracy).

Chapter 3

1. Table 3.1 shows that the cross-country mean of inflation exceeded the median for each decade. This property reflects the
skewing of inflation rates to the right, as shown in figure 3.1. That
is, there are a number of outliers with positive inflation rates of
large magnitude but none with negative inflation rates of high
magnitude. Because this skewness increased in the 1980s, the mean

inflation rate rose from the 1970s to the 1980s, although the median rate declined.

2. This estimate is similar to that reported by Fischer (1993, table 9). For earlier estimates of inflation variables in cross-country regressions, see Kormendi and Meguire (1985) and Grier and Tullock (1989).

3. To maintain comparability with previous figures, the residuals are constructed from the coefficient estimates shown in column 1 of table 1.1. However, the results are similar if the coefficients from column 1 of table 3.2 are used.

4. This system includes on the right-hand side standard deviations of inflation measured for the periods 1965–1975, 1975–1985, and 1985–1990. These variables are also included with the instruments. The findings are similar if longer-term measures of the standard deviation are used instead of the contemporaneous values.

5. Cukierman's (1992, chap. 20) results concur with this finding, especially for samples that go beyond a small number of developed countries, the kind of sample used in most of the literature on central bank independence.

6. Cukierman et al. (1993) use as instruments the turnover rate of bank governors and the average number of changes in bank leadership that occur within six months of a change in government. These measures of actual bank independence have substantial explanatory power for inflation but would not tend to be exogenous with respect to growth.

7. I have carried out SUR estimation of a panel system with the inflation rate as the dependent variable (for 1965–1975, 1975–1985, and 1985–1990), where the independent variables are lagged inflation and its square and the instrumental variables other than contemporaneous inflation used in column 1 of table 3.2. The estimated coefficient of lagged inflation is 1.47 (0.10) and that on its

square is -1.01 (0.09). No other estimated coefficients are significant at the 10 percent critical level. The R^2 values for the three periods are 0.60, 0.39, and 0.20.

8. For discussions of the CFA franc zone, see Boughton (1991) and Clement (1994). The zone maintained a fixed exchange rate with the French franc for forty-five years until the devaluation from 50 to 100 CFA francs per French franc in January 1994. At the time of the devaluation, the zone covered fourteen African countries grouped around three central banks: the West African Monetary Union of Benin, Burkina Faso, Ivory Coast, Mali, Niger, Senegal, and Togo; a group of central African countries consisting of Cameroon, Central African Republic, Chad, Congo, Equatorial Guinea, and Gabon; and the Comoros. Some original members of the zone left to establish independent currencies: Djibouti in 1949, Guinea in 1958, Mali in 1962 (until it rejoined in 1984), Madagascar in 1963, Mauritania in 1973, and the Comoros in 1981 (to set up its own form of CFA franc). Equatorial Guinea, which joined in 1985, is the only member that is not a former colony of France (and not French speaking).

9. The seven in the sample are Barbados, the Dominican Republic (attributed to France rather than Spain; see the notes to table 3.5), Guyana, Haiti, Jamaica, Surinam, and Trinidad and Tobago. Five other former British colonies in Latin America that are not in this sample—Bahamas, Belize, Grenada, St. Lucia, and St. Vincent—experienced the relatively low average inflation rate of 6.9 percent from 1970 to 1990.

10. These four are Angola, Cape Verde, Guinea-Bissau, and Mozambique. Data are unavailable for Cape Verde and Guinea-Bissau in the 1960s (prior to independence). The figures for Angola in the 1980s are rough estimates.

11. I have carried out SUR estimation of a panel system with the inflation rate as the dependent variable (for 1965–1975, 1975–1985,

and 1985–1990), where the independent variables are the instrumental variables used in column 1 of table 1.1. The estimated coefficient on the Spain-Portugal colonial dummy is 0.125 (0.027) and that on the dummy for other colonies is 0.159 (0.051). The R^2 values are 0.35 for 1965–1975, 0.09 for 1975–1985, and 0.05 for 1985–1990. Thus, inflation is difficult to explain, especially if most contemporaneous variables and lagged inflation are excluded as regressors (see note 7). Two variables that are sometimes suggested as determinants of inflation—trade openness (measured by ratios of exports and imports to GDP) and country size (measured by log of population)—are insignificant if added to the system. Years since independence also has no explanatory power for inflation. This result may arise because the former colonies of Spain and Portugal in Latin America became independent at roughly the same time.

12. In the model, the fall in the growth rate by 0.3 to 0.4 percent per year applies on impact in response to a permanent increase in the inflation rate. The growth rate would also decrease for a long time thereafter, but the magnitude of this decrease diminishes toward zero as the economy converges back to its (unchanged) long-run growth rate. Hence, in the very long run, the effect of higher inflation is a path with a permanently lower level of output, not a reduced growth rate. The numerical estimates for the reduced level of output after thirty years take account of these dynamic effects. The calculation depends on the economy's rate of convergence to its long-term growth rate (assumed, based on the empirical estimates, to be 2 to 3 percent per year). Also, the computations unrealistically neglect any responses of the other explanatory variables, such as the human capital measures and the fertility rate.

References

Aghion, Philippe, and Peter Howitt. 1992. "A Model of Growth Through Creative Destruction." *Econometrica* 60, 2 (March): 323–351.

Alesina, Alberto, and Enrico Spolaore. 1995. "On the Number and Size of Nations." Unpublished paper, Harvard University, October.

Alesina, Alberto, and Lawrence H. Summers. 1993. "Central Bank Independence and Macroeconomic Performance: Some Comparative Evidence." *Journal of Money, Credit, and Banking* 25 (May): 151–162.

Aristotle. 1932. *Politics.* Translated by H. Rackham. Cambridge, MA: Harvard University Press.

Arrow, Kenneth J. 1962. "The Economic Implications of Learning by Doing." *Review of Economic Studies* 29 (June): 155–173.

Bade, Robin, and J. Michael Parkin. 1982. "Central Bank Laws and Monetary Policy." Unpublished paper, University of Western Ontario.

Barrett, David B., ed. 1982. *World Christian Encyclopedia.* Oxford: Oxford University Press.

Barro, Robert J. 1991. "Economic Growth in a Cross Section of Countries." *Quarterly Journal of Economics* 106, 2 (May): 407–433.

Barro, Robert J., and Jong-Wha Lee. 1993. "International Comparisons of Educational Attainment." *Journal of Monetary Economics* 32 (December): 363–394.

Barro, Robert J., and Jong-Wha Lee. 1994. "Sources of Economic Growth." *Carnegie-Rochester Conference Series on Public Policy* (June): 1–46.

Barro, Robert J., and Xavier Sala-i-Martin. 1995. *Economic Growth.* New York: McGraw-Hill.

Barro, Robert J., and Xavier Sala-i-Martin. 1997. "Technological Diffusion, Convergence, and Growth." *Journal of Economic Growth* 2, 1 (March), 1–27.

Becker, Gary S., and Robert J. Barro. 1988. "A Reformulation of the Economic Theory of Fertility." *Quarterly Journal of Economics* 103, 1 (February): 1–25.

Behrman, Jere R. 1990. "Women's Schooling and Nonmarket Productivity: A Survey and a Reappraisal." Unpublished paper, University of Pennsylvania.

Benhabib, Jess, and Mark M. Spiegel. 1994. "The Role of Human Capital in Economic Development: Evidence from Aggregate Cross-Country Data." *Journal of Monetary Economics* 34, 2 (October): 143–173.

Blömstrom, Magnus, Robert E. Lipsey, and Mario Zejan. 1993. "Is Fixed Investment the Key to Economic Growth?" Working paper no. 4436. National Bureau of Economic Research, August.

Bollen, Kenneth A. 1990. "Political Democracy: Conceptual and Measurement Traps." *Studies in Comparative International Development* (Spring): 7–24.

Boughton, James M. 1991. "The CFA Franc Zone: Currency Union and Monetary Standard." Working paper no. 91/133. International Monetary Fund.

Briault, Clive. 1995. "The Costs of Inflation." *Bank of England Quarterly Bulletin* 35 (February): 33–45.

Bruno, Michael, and William Easterly. 1995. "Inflation Crises and Long-Run Growth." Working paper no. 5209. National Bureau of Economic Research, August.

Caballe, Jordi, and Manuel S. Santos. 1993. "On Endogenous Growth with Physical and Human Capital." *Journal of Political Economy* 101, 6 (December): 1042–1067.

Caselli, Francesco, Gerardo Esquivel, and Fernando Lefort. 1996. "Reopening the Convergence Debate: A New Look at Cross-Country Growth Empirics." *Journal of Economic Growth* 1, 3 (September): 363–389.

Cass, David. 1965. "Optimum Growth in an Aggregative Model of Capital Accumulation." *Review of Economic Studies* 32 (July): 233–240.

Central Intelligence Agency. 1992. *The World Factbook.* Washington D.C.: U.S. Government Printing Office.

Clement, Jean A. P. 1994. "Striving for Stability: CFA Franc Realignment." *Finance and Development* (June): 10–13.

Cukierman, Alex. 1992. *Central Bank Strategy, Credibility, and Independence.* Cambridge, MA: MIT Press.

Cukierman, Alex, Pantelis Kalaitzidakis, Lawrence H. Summers, and Steven B. Webb. 1993. "Central Bank Independence, Growth, Investment, and Real Rates." *Carnegie-Rochester Conference Series on Public Policy* 39: 95–140.

DeLong, J. Bradford, and Lawrence H. Summers. 1991. "Equipment Investment and Economic Growth." *Quarterly Journal of Economics* 106, 2 (May): 445–502.

Fischer, Stanley. 1993. "The Role of Macroeconomic Factors in Growth." *Journal of Monetary Economics* 32, 3 (December): 485–512.

Friedman, Milton. 1962. *Capitalism and Freedom.* Chicago: University of Chicago Press.

Galton, Francis. 1886. "Regression Towards Mediocrity in Hereditary Stature." *Journal of the Anthropological Institute of Great Britain and Ireland* 15: 246–263.

Galton, Francis. 1889. *Natural Inheritance.* London: Macmillan.

Gastil, Raymond D. 1991. "The Comparative Survey of Freedom: Experiences and Suggestions." In Alex Inkeles, ed., *On Measuring Democracy.* New Brunswick, N.J.: Transaction Publishers.

Gastil, Raymond D., and subsequent editors. 1982–1983 and other years. *Freedom in the World*, Westport, CT: Greenwood Press.

Grier, Kevin B., and Gordon Tullock. 1989. "An Empirical Analysis of Cross-national Economic Growth." *Journal of Monetary Economics* 24, 2 (September): 259–276.

Grilli, Vittorio, Donato Masciandaro, and Guido Tabellini. 1991. "Political and Monetary Institutions and Public Finance Policies in the Industrial Countries." *Economic Policy* 13 (October): 341–392.

Grossman, Gene M., and Elhanan Helpman. 1991. *Innovation and Growth in the Global Economy.* Cambridge, MA: MIT Press.

Hart, Peter E. 1995. "Galtonian Regression Across Countries and the Convergence of Productivity." *Oxford Bulletin of Economics and Statistics* 57, 3 (August): 287–293.

Helliwell, John F. 1994. "Empirical Linkages Between Democracy and Economic Growth." *British Journal of Political Science* 24: 225–248.

Huber, Evelyne, Dietrich Rueschemeyer, and John D. Stephens. 1993. "The Impact of Economic Development on Democracy." *Journal of Economic Perspectives* 7 (Summer): 71–85.

Huntington, Samuel P. 1991. *The Third Wave: Democratization in the Late Twentieth Century.* Norman: University of Oklahoma Press.

Inkeles, Alex. 1991. *On Measuring Democracy.* New Brunswick, N.J.: Transaction Publishers.

Islam, Nazrul. 1995. "Growth Empirics: A Panel Data Approach." *Quarterly Journal of Economics* 110, 4 (November): 1127–1170.

Jain, S. 1975. *Size Distribution of Income: A Compilation of Data.* Washington D.C.: World Bank.

Knack, Stephen, and Philip Keefer. 1995. "Institutions and Economic Performance: Cross-Country Tests Using Alternative Institutional Measures." *Economics and Politics* 7: 207–227.

Knight, Frank H. 1944. "Diminishing Returns from Investment." *Journal of Political Economy* 52 (March): 26–47.

Knight, Malcolm, Norman Loayza, and Delano Villanueva. 1993. "Testing the Neoclassical Theory of Economic Growth." *IMF Staff Papers*, 40, 3 (September): 512–541.

Kocherlakota, N. R. 1996. "Discussion of Inflation and Growth." In *Price Stability and Economic Growth.* Federal Reserve Bank of St. Louis: St. Louis.

Koopmans, Tjalling C. 1965. "On the Concept of Optimal Economic Growth." In *The Econometric Approach to Development Planning.* Amsterdam: North Holland.

Kormendi, Roger C., and Philip G. Meguire. 1985. "Macroeconomic Determinants of Growth." *Journal of Monetary Economics* 16, 2 (September): 141–163.

Lecaillon, Jacques, et al. 1984. *Income Distribution and Economic Development.* Geneva: International Labour Office.

Lipset, Seymour Martin. 1959. "Some Social Requisites of Democracy: Economic Development and Political Legitimacy." *American Political Science Review* 53: 69–105.

Lipset, Seymour Martin. 1994. "The Social Requisites of Democracy Revisited." *American Sociological Review* 59 (February): 1–22.

Lipset, Seymour Martin, Kyoung-Ryung Seong, and John Charles Torres. 1993. "A Comparative Analysis of the Social Requisites of Democracy." *International Social Science Journal* (May): 155–175.

Logue, Dennis E., and Thomas D. Willett. 1976. "A Note on the Relationship Between the Rate and Variability of Inflation." *Economica* 43: 151–158.

Lucas, Robert E., Jr. 1988. "On the Mechanics of Economic Development." *Journal of Monetary Economics* 22, 1 (July): 3–42.

Malthus, Thomas R. 1798. *An Essay on the Principle of Population.* London: W. Pickering, 1986.

Mankiw, N. Gregory, David Romer, and David N. Weil. 1992. "A Contribution to the Empirics of Economic Growth." *Quarterly Journal of Economics* 107, 2 (May): 407–437.

Mauro, Paolo. 1995. "Corruption, Country Risk, and Growth." *Quarterly Journal of Economics* 110 (October).

Mulligan, Casey B., and Xavier Sala-i-Martin. 1993. "Transitional Dynamics in Two-Sector Models of Endogenous Growth." *Quarterly Journal of Economics* 108 3 (August): 737–773.

Nelson, Richard R., and Edmund S. Phelps. 1966. "Investment in Humans, Technological Diffusion, and Economic Growth." *American Economic Review* 56, 2 (May): 69–75.

Okun, Arthur M. 1971. "The Mirage of Steady Inflation." *Brookings Papers on Economic Activity* 2: 485–498.

Perotti, Roberto. 1996. "Growth, Income Distribution, and Democracy." *Journal of Economic Growth* 1, 2 (June), 149–187.

Przeworski, Adam, and Fernando Limongi. 1993. "Political Regimes and Economic Growth." *Journal of Economic Perspectives* 7 (Summer): 51–69.

Putnam, Robert D., with Robert Leonardi and Raffaella Y. Nanetti. 1993. *Making Democracy Work: Civic Traditions in Modern Italy.* Princeton, N.J.: Princeton University Press.

Quah, Danny. 1993. "Galton's Fallacy and Tests of the Convergence Hypothesis." *Scandinavian Journal of Economics* 95, 4 (December): 427–443.

Ramsey, Frank. 1928. "A Mathematical Theory of Saving." *Economic Journal* 38 (December): 543–559.

Rebelo, Sergio. 1991. "Long-Run Policy Analysis and Long-Run Growth." *Journal of Political Economy* 99, 3 (June): 500–521.

Ricardo, David. 1817. *On the Principles of Political Economy and Taxation.* Edited by P. Sraffa. Cambridge: Cambridge University Press, 1951 ed.

Romer, Paul M. 1986. "Increasing Returns and Long-Run Growth." *Journal of Political Economy* 94, 5 (October): 1002–1037.

Romer, Paul M. 1987. "Growth Based on Increasing Returns Due to Specialization." *American Economic Review* 77, 2 (May): 56–62.

Romer, Paul M. 1990. "Endogenous Technological Change." *Journal of Political Economy* 98, 5 (October): pt. II, S71–S102.

Sachs, Jeffrey D., and Andrew M. Warner. 1995. "Natural Resource Abundance and Economic Growth." Unpublished manuscript, Harvard Institute for International Development, December.

Sah, Raaj K. 1991. "Fallibility in Human Organizations and Political Systems." *Journal of Economic Perspectives* 5 (Spring): 67–88.

Schultz, T. Paul. 1989. "Returns to Women's Education." PHRWD background paper 89/001. Washington, D.C.: World Bank, Population, Health, and Nutrition Department.

Schumpeter, Joseph A. 1934. *The Theory of Economic Development.* Cambridge, MA: Harvard University Press.

Schwartz, Anna J. 1993. "Currency Boards: Their Past, Present, and Possible Future Role." *Carnegie-Rochester Conference Series on Public Policy* 39: 147–187.

Schwarz, Gerhard. 1992. "Democracy and Market-Oriented Reform—A Love-Hate Relationship?" *Economic Education Bulletin* 32, 5 (May).

Scully, Gerald W. 1988. "The Institutional Framework and Economic Development." *Journal of Political Economy* 96, 3 (June): 652–662.

Sheshinski, Eytan. 1967. "Optimal Accumulation with Learning by Doing." In Karl Shell, ed., *Essays on the Theory of Optimal Economic Growth*, 31–52. Cambridge, MA: MIT Press.

Sirowy, Larry, and Alex Inkeles. 1990. "The Effects of Democracy on Economic Growth and Inequality: A Review." *Studies in Comparative International Development* 25 (Spring): 126–157.

Solow, Robert M. 1956. "A Contribution to the Theory of Economic Growth." *Quarterly Journal of Economics* 70, 1 (February): 65–94.

Summers, Robert, and Alan Heston. 1991. "The Penn World Table (Mark 5): An Expanded Set of International Comparisons, 1950–1988." *Quarterly Journal of Economics* 106, 2 (May): 327–368.

Summers, Robert, and Alan Heston. 1993. "Penn World Tables, Version 5.5." Available on diskette from the National Bureau of Economic Research, Cambridge, MA.

Swan, Trevor W. 1965. "Economic Growth and Capital Accumulation." *Economic Record* 32 (November): 334–361.

Tocqueville, Alexis de. 1835. *Democracy in America*. Translated by Henry Reeve. London: Saunders & Otley.

Uzawa, Hirofumi. 1965. "Optimal Technical Change in an Aggregative Model of Economic Growth." *International Economic Review* 6 (January): 18–31.

Index